Letters from Bonaire

Born and raised in New York City, Marion West graduated from New York University in English and drama before embarking on an eclectic career which included book reviewing, fashion modelling, and buying for a major cosmetics and jewelry firm. She has traveled in Europe, Canada, Mexico and the Caribbean as a Bahá'í teacher and has been active in the Bahá'í community of the United States for over forty years. Somewhere she also found the time to produce and bring up four children, and is now a grandmother of five.

Since returning from Bonaire and 'retiring' to Nevada she has become active in volunteer community work for organizations such as Cancer Drive, the Telephone Reassurance Program, and the Sierra Nevada Children's Home. She is a Director of the Boulder City Senior Center and of the Remedial School of the Rene Sparks Indian Colony.

Marion West

Letters from Bonaire

by

Marion West

GEORGE RONALD
OXFORD

GEORGE RONALD, Publisher
46 High Street, Kidlington, Oxford, OX5 2DN

British Library Cataloguing in Publication data

West Marion
Letters from Bonaire
1. Bahai life. Biographies
I. Title
297'93092

ISBN 0-85398-294-5

Printed in Great Britain by
Billing & Sons Ltd, Worcester

Contents

Acknowledgements

I want to thank my patient and wise editors, May Ballerio and Eleanor Mazidian for guiding me and reassuring me during the process of putting my experiences between the covers of a book.

Introduction

North of Caracas, Venezuela, West of Trinidad and South of Haiti lies the island of Bonaire. It is part of a group known as the Netherland Antilles, sometimes called the ABC Islands. It is less well-known than its sister islands of Aruba and Curaçao.

I did not arrive on Bonaire by plan or intent. Whether it was accident or Divine Plan I will leave to the reader to judge. It happened this way. On a bright sunny morning my husband, Tom, and I were at breakfast when a call from the US Bahá'í National Center came through. I was asked if I were free to go to Bonaire to temporarily replace the Bahá'í there who had to return to the States because of a death in her family.

I consulted with my husband. He was, as always, very supportive. Whenever I was invited to assist in the work of our Faith his answer to 'Should I go?' was always the same. He would smile and say, 'Since they asked you, can you say "No"?' He was always willing to give me freedom to serve the Cause we both loved so well. We agreed that I should go.

It was understood that I probably wouldn't have to remain on Bonaire more than three months. That was when the lady I was replacing was expected to return. We had no idea that my stay there would extend to almost a year because family problems made her return difficult.

My preparation for the journey was filled with excitement and joy. Bahá'ís believe it is a sacred privilege to share the Message of Bahá'u'lláh, the Founder of the Bahá'í Faith, with all the world. Ever since the coming of Bahá'u'lláh (1817–92), teachers have gone out from their homes to places that His Message of the oneness of God and the unity of mankind has not yet reached. These teachers are guided by the National Bahá'í Assembly of the country in which they live or visit. This institution is usually located in the capital city and has committees which assist in the various aspects of its work. My National Assembly in the United States has its center in Wilmette, Illinois; while I was living on Bonaire I was under the jurisdiction of the National Spiritual Assembly of the Bahá'ís of Venezuela, with its seat in Caracas.

When Bahá'í teachers leave their countries and travel to distant places for the purpose of sharing the Teachings of Bahá'u'lláh with others they are called 'pioneers'. Sometimes a pioneer may help other Bahá'ís become 'deepened' in their understanding of their Faith, that is, to become well-versed in its history and its teachings and be able to undertake a more profound study on their own. Pioneers do not consider themselves missionaries, although their mission is to share love and fellowship with all. Usually they are not subsidized by the Faith; they are expected to become part of the area to which they have gone by working, studying and socializing there. They go, humbly, prepared to meet and overcome obstacles in order to find those souls ready to receive the Message they have come to share. It is the aim of pioneers to become self-supporting and, as much as possible, to live in harmony with the people they have come to share their lives with.

And so it happened that on an early spring morning I set out for Bonaire on a journey which would transform my life. It was to become a journey of self-discovery, a journey of change from one spiritual condition to another. My story is the story of a change in inner condition so subtle and gradual that there was no awareness of it happening. Only in retrospect did I see the transformation which had taken place and what I had gained.

The letters which follow were written to Tom so that he might share in the wonderful adventure that his loving heart had made possible. His generous spirit caused him to duplicate each letter and send it to friends so that they too might share my experiences. The letters I received in return from these friends attested to their pleasure and excitement as they waited for news from Bonaire to arrive.

This book is dedicated to the memory of my husband, Tom West, without whose loving and complete support there would have been no Bonaire for me

P.O. Box 33
Bonaire
Netherlands Antilles

June 22, 1975

THIS is the first installment of the impressions of a really amateur pioneer. Amateur in that nothing in my life has prepared me for what I have experienced so far and for what lies ahead. None of it has been bad – just different. My flight to Miami was ordinary. It was the first time I have flown in such a huge plane and although it was billed as a 'no-frills' flight, coffee, pop and peanuts were served several times and each seat was equipped with earphones and a good choice of programs.

I was met in Miami by Peggy Stackhouse, a local Bahá'í who extended beautiful and gracious hospitality to me, a complete stranger according to the reckoning of the world but a dear and welcoming sister according to the spirit of our Faith. She drove me to the airport the next morning and it was then that my pioneer journey began. I boarded an ALM plane and was immediately in another world. Most of the passengers spoke another language – the stewardesses spoke several but were not really comfortable in English. My seat companion was a lovely little girl, about nine, who was traveling between Miami, where she spent several months with her mother, and Guyana, where she lived several months with her father. She was a very precocious child and we amused one another for the four hours of the flight. I left her at the airport in Curaçao where again I was met by a Bahá'í sister, Dr Nosrat Rabbani. This extraordinary woman is a Persian, a medical doctor working with the Dutch government in public health service; she is also the doctor who accompanied Rúḥíyyih Khánum for three months of an expedition on the Amazon rivers. I stayed with her at her home for two and a half marvelous days.

I met with the Regional Committee which directs the teaching of the Bahá'í Faith on Bonaire, Aruba and Curaçao; attended an introductory talk on the Faith given for the public and delivered in Dutch by a Persian Bahá'í and, unbelievable as it sounds, understood every word he said. I was surprised at one point to find myself nodding my head in absolute agreement with a wonderful point he was making. He is an Auxiliary Board Member named Mas'úd Mázgání and he is so great I wanted to be where he is and begin learning all over again.

I felt so terribly small and unknowing. I'm only beginning to know what 'humble' means. He had been in Bonaire the week before I got there and had been to the house I will live in. His description of it left me weak and I wanted to run away from it, but the thought of my beautiful hostess and her stories of what she and Rúḥíyyih Khánum put up with on that Amazon trip made me ashamed. My bravado sounded false, even to me, when I said, 'Oh well, if others can do it, so can I.'

From Curaçao I flew in a tiny little plane to Bonaire. There were only seven passengers and it was necessary to climb a rope ladder to get in. I sat right behind the pilots and practically in their laps, which wouldn't have been too bad considering that they were very young and handsome kids! The entire flight was less than 20 minutes and we flew low enough so that I felt as if I were skimming the Caribbean Sea. At the airport I went through customs and was passed through like magic when I said I was the Bahá'í friend of Rhoda Vaughn. I took a taxi to the Hotel Bonaire where I introduced myself to the blackest, most radiant, warm-hearted woman I have ever met, Mrs Pieters. She isn't even remotely interested in the Faith – she's too busy living the most robust, materialistic life you can imagine. She is, however, a jewel and a powerful and influential friend whose friendship I am blessed to have. I was supposed to stay with her for a few days, at seven guilders a day (about US$4) but because of the condition of my house the few days is extended to ten, which puts a big dent in my resources of only US$210.

The house had been closed up for some time since Rhoda left the Island. There were spiders, scorpions, roaches as big as mice, and only God knows what else. I didn't stay around long enough to find out. There is a really nice kitchen – that is, it has a great double stainless steel sink, a large refrigerator with freezer section, a door that opens onto the back porch, and a large window over the sink. But that is it. No stove is in evidence nor cupboards nor any kind of storage space. The bed is a four-inch foam rubber mat on a wooden platform about four inches from the floor. I had visions of the bed partners I could expect and said, 'No thank you – not for me.' Even the thought of the hammock the doctor and Rúḥíyyih Khánum used on the barge seemed preferable.

It took all of the ten days to get the house fumigated, exterminated, scrubbed from ceiling to floor. I bought a small three-burner gas stove – the table-top kind – with no oven for about US$40. I paid US$9.50 for my first tank of cooking gas and sweated it out until it was connected. I am learning a beautiful, radiant kind of patience, which no one who knows me will believe. However, even as I write that I'm wondering how much patience was involved and how much dread at having to move over there. At Mrs Pieters' house, which is situated on a main road over which all of Bonaire passes at one time or another, there lives a Jamaican family – father, who works for Chicago Bridge Company building oil tanks for Shell; mother, a 'Jesus-saved-me' Christian; and two small boys aged ten and twelve. There is always someone to talk to and laugh with; people are constantly dropping in to visit. It is a lively household and I know I shall miss it. On the other hand, it is not as clean as I would have it; there are three miserable dogs and mice. So all things balance out – my house will be spotlessly clean and pest-free, if my determination and efforts can make it so, but it will be lonesome.

Bonaire is a strange little island – solid rock with a soil covering of not more than six inches, at least in the area where I am. It is really a coral reef, 40 miles long and 5 miles wide.

The population is about 8000, mostly blacks, descendants of those brought here by the Dutch in the

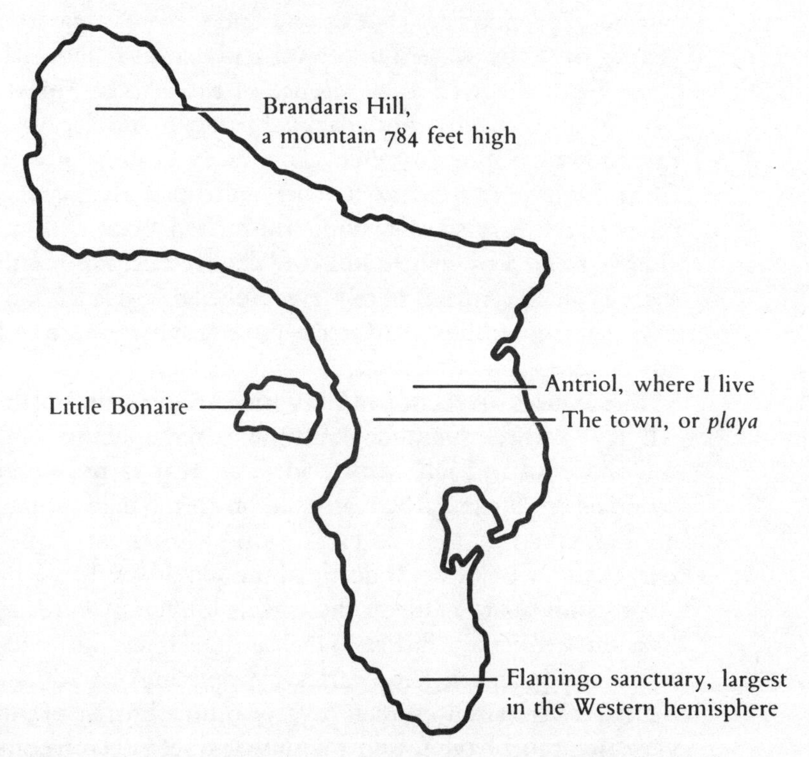

1600s. There were some Indians here at that time but not very many. They were pretty well killed off by the Spanish who discovered the island in 1499. The blacks intermarried with these and there is evidence of this in some who have dark skins and African features with straight hair. The main industry was panning salt. Recently Shell Oil has installed storage tanks and is employing many people, in addition to the great numbers who are brought in by American companies working on building the tanks. The air is pure and unpolluted; the water is converted seawater which is purified and good. It tastes good and sweet; it is better tasting than any water I have ever had except that which came from the well at the house of the Báb in Shíráz. The weather is hot and sticky but there is always a breeze which brings relief. The wind comes mostly from the east and I am extremely fortunate in that my house faces east so the living room and bedroom are always fanned by gentle and cooling breezes. Although there is an electric fan here I have not had to use it. I am told that September and October are scorchers here so I am keeping the fan handy.

The houses all seem to follow one architectural plan. All have a porch (veranda) of stone or tile opening onto a living room. Each front door, when it is not solid wood as are those in the really old houses, has two glass doors flanked by glass louvers. I don't know any other way to describe these. Indeed, all the windows throughout the house are made of these glass louvers. There are two sets to each window panel and each works independently giving a wide variety of openings or adjustments. There are no screens except on the homes of the very rich but I have found a way that screens can be put on my windows and if I can afford it, I will have it done. Even the smallest house seems to have the amenity of a dining room. Inside plumbing is the rule, with showers instead of tubs. Except in the richest homes there is no hot water. Indeed, in my house there is only one faucet in the sink and one in the shower. Mornings and evenings the water is cool, never cold. It comes from huge storage tanks and is warmed by the sun. In the afternoon and early evening on most days you can enjoy a reasonably hot shower, but I have come to really like the cool morning and evening ones.

My house is situated on a dirt road, a short-cut from the main road. There is the home and workshop of an auto mechanic directly in front. Immediately to my left is a jerry-made house. It was really 'made' in the sense that it wasn't 'built'. It was thrown together of odd pieces of whatever came to hand. The roof is made of pieces of tin hammered flat and somehow held together. Directly behind and a little to the left is the house of a man who has fourteen children and countless relatives who come to call. Sometimes a bunch arrive before any others leave and your guess is as good as mine about how they bed them down!

The Bonairians are delightful, full of fun and jokes, honest and clean. They are so proud when you profess to like their little step-sister of an island. Many I have met speak some English but are delighted that I want to speak their language, Papiamentu, with them.

There is a joke through the island about me. I met a sweet old man (86) who did a lot of work for Rhoda. His name is Carlos Mercera and he looks about 60 and acts like 40. He is helping me get the house together. I met him my second day on the island when I had already acquired a pretty good Papiamentu vocabulary. I spoke to him and he answered by rattling off a stream while I sputtered and laughed and said, 'Nada mas, pa fabor. Mi ta sina Papiamentu, solamente.' ('No more, please. I am only learning Papiamentu.') He howled and said, 'Then you shouldn't speak it so good. You deceived me.' His English is very good. He lived in New Jersey for several years. He is one of my best friends and although he has made it quite clear that he isn't interested in the Faith, he is nevertheless willing to help me spread it in any way he can.

Shopping is difficult for me. I am not able to translate guilders, or 'florins' as the natives call them, into dollars so that I can determine if I can afford to buy something. So far my meals have consisted mostly of delicious Dutch cheese, bread, cucumbers, green peppers and tuna. I did buy a package of frozen fillet of flounder and one of frozen spinach and had a good meal out of that. There is no buttermilk or yogurt that I have yet found. I can get whole milk although it is very expensive. Most people here use powdered milk which they buy in huge cans. I am so glad I brought 100 yogurt tablets with me; they will keep my insides in good working order.

Dogs, chickens, and goats are everywhere. Sleeping is made very difficult because every house has several large dogs which sleep outdoors and each considers it his sole duty to protect the premises which results in a barking contest every time either a person or an animal approaches a house. Each dog seems set to prove that his bark is the loudest and most ferocious, although really all the dogs I have encountered are sweet-tempered and lovable. They don't really scare anybody but they sure make a racket trying. At 5:00 a.m. the roosters begin and don't let up all day. They are bossy and obnoxious and I would wish them all on some rotisserie.

I am really very happy. I came here not only to teach but to learn. I have the feeling that my teaching won't really begin until I have learned some more. The only thing I am trying to do right now is to make friends. As soon as possible after my house is made ready I will try to invite some ladies in for coffee. I have some other plans which I will tell about in the next installment. Indeed, I have so much to tell that I shall keep everyone busy reading. I can only wish that you would do as much for me. I cannot tell you how I walk every day to the Post Office and pray as I open my box that there will be a letter from one of you. Now I understand the plea of the pioneers for letters from home. Please help fill my mail box and my heart with your precious letters.

June 23

I'M afraid I may be a little muddle-headed this morning. Sleep was impossible last night, for some of the neighbors had a party. Almost any occasion is cause for a party – a noisy one which lasts well into the morning of the next day. Since houses are clustered in neighborhoods, one party is everyone's party. Liquor flows freely. I cannot say that inhibitions are relaxed because these are the least inhibited people one could imagine, but I may safely say that caution is thrown to the winds. I think it is not a disparagement of Bonairians to say that they are amoral. It is not unusual for a woman to have had 12 to 14 children with three or four different men. I know one man, a most highly respected man known for his generosity and helpfulness, who is the father of 24 children – that he knows of and supports. He will laughingly tell you that he has sired 'only the Lord knows how many others'. Unmarried pregnancies are no shame but the Dutch government has ordered that a man who impregnates a girl must marry her or go to jail. There is no incidence of rape on the island and foreign young men are quickly made aware of the law, so while there is plenty going on in the bushes, the results are not socially disastrous. Because everything is so open and because there seems to be so much respect for human dignity, this is probably one of the 'safest' places in the world. You see, it is urban. That is to say, the island is really one big city although very unsophisticated and unmechanized. 'Things' haven't yet taken possession of the people so there is very little thieving. Sex is easy – so no rape. Frequent parties and dances, lots of good-natured scuffling, and loud, good-humored arguing, all of which let off steam so that violence is unnecessary. I hope I am not implying that this is Eden. There is a good and well-trained police force of some 30 men who wouldn't be needed if the island were the Olympus of the gods, but compared to most anyplace else the living here is good and easy.

When I first saw my house I was disheartened. It is so bare and unlovely. If I had more money I could fix it up to make it very attractive. All the walls are painted white – which is great – except one in the living room and one in the dining room. These are a disgusting red-orange, ugly as a mustache on the Mona Lisa. If I could afford it I would have them repainted. I'll have to find some way to cover them; they give off awful vibes. As I mentioned, the bed in the house is a pallet on the floor but since there are lizards, mice and ants, I have no intention of sleeping with them and am arranging to borrow a bedstead and springs. There are hundreds of small lizards in the fields. Strange as it seems, I am neither frightened nor disgusted by them. They are really rather pretty and very playful. I don't mind watching them – from a considerable distance of course. I understand there are also large iguana lizards which the islanders catch and eat and consider quite a delicacy. I haven't seen one yet and would just as soon not. There are hundreds of goats and they roam freely like cattle. They are very small and dainty with sweet faces and varied and beautiful colors. I am told that their meat is very tender and lean like lean lamb. I know I shall try it soon.

Tuesday, June 24

AFTER watching them bring in a slaughtered goat – throat slit, head and horns black and bloody – and after smelling the smell of the hair and top skin being singed off and hearing the scrape-scrape of the knife and choking on the thick, heavy smell of it cooking, I doubt I'll ever try goat meat – no matter how sweet they say it is. If God tests us to make strengths out of our weaknesses, I'm afraid I'll give Him a full-time job.

Sunday night I went to a church service with Mrs Reed, the Jamaican lady who, with her husband and two small sons, lives at the house where I am staying. She has been 'saved by the precious blood of the Lamb', is a hymn-singing, close-minded gal but rather pleasant and company for me. Any mention of the Faith and she tightens up and becomes defensive so I don't talk about it at all. I'm sure she intended to save my soul when she invited me to attend services with her. Trans World Radio – a radio church of the air – has one of its largest transmitters on Bonaire. They have a large permanent staff, mostly Americans. There are currently about forty-five families and the Sunday services are mainly for them. They don't really do much proselytizing of the native people. They are rather clannish and make no effort to learn the local language. They are, indeed, rather negative about it – 'Let them speak Spanish.' Mrs Reed heard them broadcast in Jamaica and was delighted to learn that they held services here. Their service is simple – much singing and, of course, 'Jesus is the rock of my salvation' and 'There is no other one but Jesus' is the whole theme. They are strictly fundamentalist and Paulian and you can see them anguishing over my 'foolishness'. I went to please Mrs Reed and to meet people but I found their world closed to me. I am not 'one of them'.

I have made one very interesting friend – a handsome young Bonairian, about 22, who works at the Bank. He seems to have a really ready, open mind. He is eager for much contact with me in order to polish his English. He has a feel for fine language and is not satisfied with 'tourist English'. I pray that his friendship with me will ripen into love for Bahá'u'lláh. He would be a jewel and I think he is strong enough to stand any backlash.

My young friend's name is Raphael Statie (pronounced 'Stahsee'). He says he will arrange for a showing of any Bahá'í films we can get from the Regional Teaching Committee and that he knows some young people who will come when my house is in order. I will also invite several ladies to come to visit – just to visit – and see what comes of it. These people offer their friendship so readily and generously that I feel constrained not to abuse it or take advantage of it. You see, I am learning patience.

Every day I walk to town – or *playa* (literally 'beach', but that's where the town is) – and do a little shopping. I try to buy a little in each shop so that I will get known. I buy bug spray here, nail enamel remover there, someplace else I buy talcum powder, etc. I can get almost anything I need here on Bonaire but I limit my wants to my budget.

I must confess to dreading to move from Mrs Pieters'. My house is far from town – a really long walk. I will be lonesome and since I discovered that there are scorpions as well as lizards, mice and roaches, I dread having to cope with them myself. Rhoda left two cats and I shall feed them and cultivate them, hoping they will drive off small things. Before I move in I shall spray and fumigate and close up the place for a day hoping to start clean and then pray my heart out that I may have no more unwelcome visitors than I can handle. I am hardly the stuff a pioneer is made of and I pray that my squeamishness doesn't prevent me from doing a good job. I am ashamed to confess that I would want to be ensconced in the air-conditioned, immaculate comfort of the Hotel Bonaire, enjoying the beautiful private beach – which is not really private, they permit its use by everyone – and knowing that, if by chance a crawly appeared, I'd only have to call the desk and help would arrive. But this cannot be and from somewhere I'll find the strength and courage to handle it. In the meantime I am resting and relaxing for the first time in my life. I have lots of time to write and to read and I'm doing just that.

Friday, June 27

ASIDE from all the obvious changes in my life, I think

the greatest has been learning to sit – just sit. I have settled into a kind of routine (how deadly that would have sounded once!). I wake about 6:00 a.m. and, after doing all the usual morning things, I have a light breakfast of tea, bread and cheese, sometimes orange juice or a fruit. At about 8:30 I walk to town, about a mile or a mile and a half away. I have had Mrs Reed as a walking partner and we talk of many things as we walk. We are well known by the people who live on the various roads we take on the way from house to *playa*. We like to vary the route so that every day seems an adventure. She tells me that our daily excursions cause a lot of talk. It is rare to see a white American lady walking out with a lady of color on such obviously friendly terms. At first it was thought that I was a rich American lady with my servant but when it was seen that I carried my own shopping bag and that as often as not she preceded me into a store that idea was abandoned. As the store-keepers and people we would stop to talk to on the road began to know us they accepted the idea that we are friends and equals. She tells me that I am much loved by the people for this. Instead of making me happy that made me sad – sad to think that such a relationship had to be considered unusual.

We usually walk from one end of the *playa* to the other. We stop at the pier and see if we can buy something from the boats . . . we want to be tempted but rarely are. Then we go to the Post Office and my day is really off to a good start when I find something in my box. The Postmaster has become a good friend and never fails to come out to greet me and ask if I'm all right or if I need anything. We then go to the bank – if I need money, which is often because I cash only small checks. I'm afraid of spending too much and it's easy when you can't think in guilders. Anyway, this gives me a chance to say, 'Bon dia' to all my friends at the bank and 'Pasa bon' when I leave. We sometimes go to the bakery and get freshly-baked brown bread – *pan brun* – which is delicious and cheap. A small loaf costs 65 cents Dutch or about 38 cents American. I have discovered that the ice cream store (and they have marvelous real ice cream as well as soft ice cream) will get plain yogurt for me. They get it every Wednesday and it is thick and wonderful-tasting. So every Wednesday we will make that stop. Then we go to the supermarket. This is just as well stocked as any of ours and has just about the same things. A problem sometimes arises because many of the goods come from Holland and I cannot read the labels well enough to find what I want. What I find hardest to accept are the prices of most things. I can assure you that my menus are most modest. Meat here, though, is great. Beef is Colombian or Venezuelan – lean yet tender – and I can get beef tenderloin for US$2.00 a pound and once in a while I shall. By 10:30 we are ready to walk home – if we are not laden down with packages. If we are we hail a taxi. If Mrs Reed does it, we ride home for one guilder or about 60¢ our money; if I call the taxi he charges five guilders. You see, Americans are rich. But even at one guilder we do not do this often. We both enjoy the walk and need the exercise because once we get home the sitting begins. I have read a book a day since I've been here. Mrs Pieters has a fantastic library of paperbacks. I could read a book a day all the while I'm on Bonaire and not exhaust her supply. I have written letters and cards to everyone. I shampoo every other day and shower three times a day. I've done my nails just about every day, pray and still find time to sit and sit and sit. Mostly I sit on the veranda and watch the trees across the road dance in the wind. I have seen at least seventeen varieties of birds, and lizards of every size from 2½ inches to a foot long. I've watched herds of goats daintily and cautiously run through the field across the way and all the while people are passing either on foot or in cars. Everyone waves and smiles. Occasionally someone comes over and talks – just passing the time of day – there always seems to be time for a small exchange. I eat when I'm hungry and very simply. These Jamaicans, who by their own admission 'live to fill their bellies', are afraid I'm starving myself but that is not so. My grocery bills attest to that. I usually have dinner about 7:00 – or even 8:00 – so the evening won't seem so long. The two little boys, Mrs Pieters and I watch TV from 8:30 to 9:30. At 10:00 I go to bed after a delicious cold shower. See – already a big change is observed. That the day would come when I would consider a cold shower delicious should reveal something. When I move into my house I doubt that the pattern will vary very much except that I hope I will have visitors. I shall try to work my budget so that I can serve nice things. It is not only to a man's heart that we go through the belly but to the hearts of Bonairian women as well.

I would like to teach the children English. There are dozens of children near my house. The father of the family of fourteen, Papa Diek (Dutch for fat or thick), speaks English and has been very helpful to me but his children speak only Papiamentu or Dutch. Dutch is the official language of the Islands and is the language spoken in the schools.

Saturday, June 28

I HAVE just had a minor revelation. We are so rich in the number of prayers revealed by the Central Figures of our Faith, and yet some reach us and touch us more intimately and meaningfully than others. I had often wondered why I wasn't getting more out of the prayers. I think I now understand. In His tender and all-knowing mercy God has prepared for our unknown and unsuspected needs and in the storehouse of His divine medicine chest is already stored whatever we shall need. The prayers are there awaiting our need for them. For years I had dutifully read all the teaching prayers without real comprehension of what some of them were saying, particularly this one:

Whoever sets out on a teaching journey to any place; let him recite this prayer day and night during his travels in foreign lands.

O GOD, my God! Thou seest me enraptured and

attracted toward Thy glorious kingdom, enkindled with the fire of Thy love amongst mankind, a herald of Thy kingdom in these vast and spacious lands, severed from aught else save Thee, relying on Thee, abandoning rest and comfort, remote from my native home, a wanderer in these regions, a stranger fallen upon the ground, humble before Thine exalted Threshold, submissive toward the heaven of Thine omnipotent glory, supplicating Thee in the dead of night and at the break of dawn, entreating and invoking Thee at morn and at eventide to graciously aid me to serve Thy Cause, to spread abroad Thy Teachings and to exalt Thy Word throughout the East and the West.

O Lord! Strengthen my back, enable me to serve Thee with the utmost endeavor, and leave me not to myself, lonely and helpless in these regions.

O Lord! Grant me communion with Thee in my loneliness, and be my companion in these foreign lands.

Verily, Thou art the Confirmer of whomsoever Thou willest in that which Thou desirest, and, verily, Thou art the All-Powerful, the Omnipotent.

'Abdu'l-Bahá

But out here – really alone, a stranger entering upon a new life, praying constantly for strength and assistance – I know so well that anything I may do to serve and assist His Cause can only be through His Grace. Here there are no precedents to follow, no rules to go by. Any little mistake here can be serious. One feels so terribly inadequate, especially one who has relied on the quick, rational answer, the power of a logical explanation. When communication must be by simple, short phrases, by gestures and even by silence, when all the well-used clichés, analogies and examples fail, then one begins to realize what absolute dependence on the outpourings of the Holy Assistance is. This prayer so fills my need and says in precious words what my heart cries.

This morning we went to the *playa* and then took a taxi to my house. It has been cleaned and the refrigerator emptied of stuff left months ago. It has been scrubbed and disinfected. I bought a lot of groceries and stocked it pretty well. I spent all the money I'll be able to until my next Social Security check. I need storage shelves or cupboards or something in which to store canned goods, jars, household supplies, etc. There are none – and I mean NONE – no cupboards, closets or chests of any kind in the house except a small area under the sink. The sink is a beauty – double stainless steel basins and drain board, deep and wonderfully usable. I will need curtains. It's like living in a fish tank – windows on all sides from ceiling almost to floor. There should be screens, at least for bedroom and kitchen. US$100 would probably do the whole thing though I dare not spend that much. But the house is clean and I think by constant vigilance I can keep it bug-free. It will be a battle but I'm ready.

I had unpacked some of Rhoda's things and found a couple of good pots, some linen, a few dishes and enough cutlery. I'm sure I can get by with these. I had to buy a mirror – there was not one in the house anywhere. Imagine a woman without a mirror! I expect to move in Monday if my gas stove is connected. To save the US$20 or so that it would have cost to connect the tank of bottled gas, Papa Diek, my neighbor, has offered to do it. He has the meter and the pipes but no one rushes to do anything here and it's a matter of just waiting until it gets done. (See? Patience again!) The tank of gas cost 17 guilders (US$9) and will probably last two months. Mrs

Reed and the boys went to the house with me and we walked back here to Mrs Pieters'. It was a long, hot walk, part of it on a dirt road that ran through a cactus forest. Long, spiny cactus as tall as trees grow close to the road and it is said that the iguana lives here. We all pretended to be so brave – but we made a lot of noise and did a lot of hysterical laughing and walked a little faster than normal. It really wasn't bad once we reached the paved road and we realized how silly we had been. It's funny, though, that even a simple little thing like this becomes an adventure and breaks the monotony of the long, quiet day. It is something to laugh about and talk about. But with whom will I laugh and talk after I move over? I almost dread going.

July 2

I MOVED into my house two days ago. I slept wonderfully well that night with no fears, no uncertainty – I was really home. The little house has a good feel. It's as clean as it can possibly be. When I first saw it I said, 'Who can live without a closet, a cupboard, a chest of drawers, someplace to put things?' The answer is – I CAN! I'm learning about mixed blessings. You see, without closets, etc. there is no place for 'things' to hide and breed. Everything is out in the open. I can attack anything before it attacks me. I'm delighted at not having closets. I'm also learning how prayers are answered. I prayed so hard to be able to cope with bugs; all I asked was to be made unafraid and strong enough to handle 'creatures'. It works out that I may never have to. Every night before I go to sleep I spray the kitchen and the bathroom and in the morning I sweep out whatever there may be. During the day when I leave the house I spray the bedroom, living, and dining rooms. I know all about the dangers of sprays but until I learn how to be a 'pioneer' I'll spray and be happy. What would just be an annoyance to a more sensible person is to me a major crisis and probably the heaviest cross I'll have to bear.

My stove works beautifully. I have stocked the refrigerator and bought staples like rice, corn meal, etc. and I'm ready for my first dinner guest – Carlos Mercera. He's that dear old man who has been so kind to me. He was here early Tuesday morning worried that I might have been afraid and slept badly. He is coming this afternoon to paint one of the two dining-room chairs. He'll do the other one tomorrow. I asked him to stay for dinner and I think he was pleased.

I have developed a routine here too. Mornings are cool and lovely so I try to do housework things. This morning I washed and waxed the living room floor, hung some pictures, finished finding places to put my things, started dinner, fed the cats. This lasted until about 10:30. I showered, shampooed my hair and set it, fixed lunch and prayed some more. This praying is different from any I've ever done. For the first time in my life I know how utterly dependent I am. Nothing that I know, none of my talents, whatever they may be, are useful here. And so I pray for guidance, for wisdom and tact and the patience that I will need.

I must tell you about the cats. There is a mother cat, small, white mostly with splashed-on black spots. She has the eyes of a child – so large, so luminous, so searching. She had two kittens. When I first saw them it was obvious that one was sick and I hated myself for not being able to pick it up and do something for it. Carlos, who was with me, was very unconcerned. The next day he told me that the kitty was dead and he had buried it. He said he would have thrown it in the field except he had seen the look on my face and knew I wouldn't have liked that. How perceptive this rare old man is. The other kitty I love. It is a grey, black and white tiger – the kind my children always used to have. It's very playful but wild and frightened of me. It was born and raised as a wild thing without the smell or touch of humans. The mother does probably remember because she is less timid. Although I'm not the greatest animal lover in the world I couldn't resist those eyes and, though I don't let them in the house, I do talk to them and make efforts at playing with them. The mother suffers me to stroke her and will even rub up against me but kitty is still wary. The mother climbs up on the window at night while I am reading and just watches me. I feed them twice a day – they're both so skinny – and they come running from far off in the fields when I open the back door. They seem to keep the lizards away because I've seen only a few of them whereas at Mrs Pieters' they actually seemed to swarm in spite of the dogs.

Every afternoon I write letters or keep an account of the day's events. I don't think I'll go to town too often. It's a pretty long walk and I spend money every time I go. I've given up going to the Post Office every day because I don't like the disappointment of the empty box. I have a good radio here. It is Rhoda's. But there is so little worth listening to. Every afternoon I can usually get some good classical music but the rest of the time is filled with several Church of the Air stations or programs in Spanish. If we in the States are annoyed with the length and number of commercials, we'd go crazy here. No musical selection is played all the way through without interruption. It is always cut short for the commercial which seems interminable. Spanish disc jockeys are loud, raucous and, to make it worse, there are usually two who interrupt each other and try to outshout each other. Even the 'beat' which I thought I liked gets wearing. I tried listening, hoping to pick up my Spanish, but Spanish-speaking announcers speak as rapidly as English-speaking ones and they go on longer.

July 4

It has been raining and it is wonderful. I was preparing to walk to the *playa* when quite suddenly the sky greyed – it doesn't get black here, just a solid covering of thick grey that makes a low, heavy ceiling overhead – and as I was debating my trip the ceiling opened up and fell in one giant swoosh. It poured with the fury of an angry, hurt lover and subsided, all contrition and gentleness with the promise of later delights. That's the way it is here. Even Nature regrets her bad temper and knocks herself out to make it up. This has been the second day of the rains. They began Wednesday night about 11:00 and I understood why the houses are concrete block and solid as the earth itself. Nothing else could stand up to the fury of a tropical downpour. But even at its worst it smelled so good. It poured most of the night and began again yesterday morning at about 9:00, but when it cleared in the afternoon the sky was the gentlest, sweetest blue; the breeze was pungently perfumed (it is desert, you know) and the air was crystal-clear. I breathe the air the way I drink the water; it has a taste and quality that I had forgotten existed and I can't seem to get enough of either.

I have had two wonderful days. Wednesday evening I had a dinner guest, my old friend Carlos Mercera. Dinner was good and this old gentleman has class. He was born on Bonaire but had been away for 58 years. Most of his life he has been at sea. Even after he married an American girl and established a home in New Jersey, he still went to sea. He certainly had very few cultural 'advantages' and yet his manners are impeccable. He is really something. Old age becomes something to look forward to with eager anticipation, not dread, if it can be like his.

After sincere and gracious thank-yous and at a proper time he left and I settled down for a quiet evening alone. An hour or so later a car stopped outside and I went to ask who it was.

'It's the Postmaster. I have brought my wife to meet you.'

'Bon bini, bon bini,' I replied. (Welcome, welcome.)

'She speaks English,' said Mr Martis.

They had with them four of their five children. These were the four younger ones; the oldest is away at school in Curaçao. The baby is less than two years old and adorable. The others were shy and sweet and soon we were warm friends. Mr Martis is rather fair-skinned, more Mexican looking. Stella, his wife, is very dark with fine features. The children vary in shade but are generally fairer than the mother. Genetic studies of these people should prove very interesting. These were my first real visitors and I shall always feel very tenderly about them for that act of thoughtfulness and friendship.

Last night I had another wonderful surprise. I was just

finishing my dinner at about 7:30 when I heard a honk outside. It was my young friend (they really are either too young or too old) Raphael from the bank. He is the President of the Centro di Bario – the Community Center – of Antriol and he had to go and open the Center and let the people know that the evening's workshop was being cancelled. He had arranged for a lady to come from Curaçao twice a week to teach a class in nail and string design but the ferry from Curaçao had been cancelled and she wouldn't be there. He asked me if I would like to go with him and afterwards he would take me for a drive and show me the island from the top of the mountain. He said that Bonaire from that height was breathtaking. I stacked the dishes in the sink and away we went. We went to the ferry first just to be sure that it wasn't coming and then to the Center. This is a very modern, well-equipped building with a large and efficient kitchen, a hall large enough to seat a couple of hundred theatre-style or a hundred for dinner and two large rooms for office and/or class rooms or conference rooms. It was built by the Government and there are four others on the island, one in each district or county.

July 4 – later

I SAW a little deeper into the nature of the Bonairian last night. When Raphael and I arrived at the Center there were about a dozen people waiting outside the locked gate. Some were rather old women and they had all evidently walked because there was no sign of cars or bicycles. After Raphael had explained, there were none of the expected murmurs of displeasure, no 'gosh' or 'for heaven's sake'; nothing but acceptance and understanding and even sympathy for Raphael for having to bring bad news. They just quietly walked away. We waited for about an hour during which time many came and left. We locked the Center and went for a look at the city by night. The drive was exciting, for after all this was a very young man at the wheel and he knew that tortuous road up the mountain as well as I know the way from my front to back door. It surprises me that I can say 'mountain' without wanting to smile. On an island like this – flat, desert and rock – that 700+ feet is indeed a 'mountain'. The road up is single lane, winding and rather steep, and even at night I could see that it was beautiful. The vegetation is different from down below; the trees are not as dwarfed and bushy but more like real trees. I knew I would want to come here in daylight. We parked the car at the top and got out. It was very dark because at this time of year the moon doesn't come up until about 2:00 in the morning; however the sky was heavily studded with stars, some so close as to look unreal. Raphael led me a little distance to a stone bench and, proudly and with an air of owning it all, bade me look upon his island. We were overlooking the harbor on the west side of the island with Kralendijk, the main city, just below. The lights of the city and the piers along the waterfront were really pretty to see but I couldn't help wondering what this beautiful, relatively unspoiled boy would say to Glitter Gulch in Las Vegas or even the view of Reno as I have seen and loved it from the rise east of the city at night. As I think back, my single greatest reaction is that I was completely unafraid. I wasn't afraid of the breakneck speed of the drive, the precariousness of our perch on the mountain edge, of crawlies, of anything – as I haven't been afraid of anything since I moved to my house. How can fear disappear, except that this is what I have been praying for – to have courage and strength. If this is indeed a gift, I hope it hasn't just been loaned to me for here and that I will lose it when I leave. I have never known such calm, peaceful acceptance of myself, my life, people and things around me. Is it possible that it was for this that I was brought to Bonaire? I haven't been this 'self' long enough to know that it will last – but while I am this ME I like it and very much want to stay this way.

We sat on that mountain top for about 20 minutes and then drove the length of the island. Raphael promised to bring me back up the mountain in the daylight but he said he wanted me to see it the way he loves it best. Before he took me home he took me to his parents' house. He wanted me to meet them. I was surprised to discover that he also lived in Antriol. I had imagined from his exquisite manners, his extraordinarily good taste in clothing, his bearing, that he was the son of very wealthy parents. This is far from the case. His mother is Bonairian, his father Venezuelan. The mother is an ample woman, taller than I and heavier but not fat. Her skin is quite dark but soft and chocolatey with features fine and clear. She is a really handsome woman. She wore a plain cotton house dress and had bare feet in the style of the islanders. Although she had obviously not been expecting me, I doubt whether she would have been different if she had: a simple, honest person. The father had owned a sailing boat from which he peddled foodstuffs from Venezuela to the islands. He would load up with plantain, bananas, avocados and other vegetables and foods in Venezuela then tie up to a pier and sell his stock from the boat. I told you how Mrs Reed and I would go down to the pier to be tempted! Mr Statie's boat sank off the coast of Venezuela and, since it was not adequately insured, he lost everything. Now he is a fisherman. The mother and two daughters bake fancy cakes and pastries at home for additional income. The older daughter works at the Ford agency here. Raphael works at the bank. Both of the younger girls babysit also and that's how they live. We visited for about one and a half hours and, although neither mother nor father speaks English and my Papiamentu is absolutely rudimentary, we got along fine. Occasionally Raphael would translate but mostly we just made ourselves understood. Raphael said it first when he came to get me and, when he mentioned it to his family, they all agreed that the name Marion or even Miriam, which is my passport name, is much too formal. They quickly collaborated and came up with the name by which I shall henceforth be known, at least to that family – Mimi! The father offered to bring me some fish from his next catch and I had to confess that I had never handled a whole fish in my life; that if I had to look at the head of a fish, open one up, scrape it or whatever it is one does to a whole raw fish, I would have to eliminate that food from my diet.

They all laughed and Raphael said, 'But my father will clean it for you and even take away the bones and give you just the meat. Will you take it then? You will, won't you, Papa?' He repeated this in Spanish to his father. Papa clapped his hands and nodded his head. I always knew I didn't have to be afraid that my many strong food prejudices would turn people off – indeed they are amused and feel that I'm a picky little child who has to be protected and spoiled – and that's the way I want it. It gives them a feeling of being, at least in this area, superior to me and makes them more kindly disposed towards me. It may be a nasty little trick but it works and, instead of alienating people from me, it endears me to them. At least it seems to work with simple, pure people.

July 5
5:00 p.m.

I WOKE early this morning as usual and, since I wasn't going to town to shop, I knew I'd have a long, long day to use. I finished washing and waxing all the floors and all those other nice housewifely things that really didn't have to be done but were time-consuming and not entirely useless. I made a big production of lunch; more time consumed. You see, I'm not saying wasted because 'wasting' time would be inexcusable; therefore the euphemistic 'consumed', O.K.? At about 2:30 p.m. I was at the wall-climbing stage and, even though it was at the hottest part of the day when the sun was really laying it on, I decided to take a walk. I had not yet walked to Mrs Pieters' alone and the thought came to me that it had been very nice to put on paper that I was now without fear, and that I felt so secure and safe, but would I really stand the test? What better way to test my new-found courage than to walk through the cactus forest, the home of the iguana, alone? I truly and honestly meant to do just that and I truly and honestly walked in that direction! It was hot but, as always, there was the ever-blowing breeze so it was not uncomfortable. There wasn't a soul around and I was reminded of 'mad dogs and Englishmen' and thought that it must certainly apply to American ladies too.

I walked happily and serenely and unafraid – but I didn't get the chance to test my strength because I got lost! Tom has often said I couldn't find my way out of a paper bag and this proved it. I had walked right by the road where I was supposed to turn off to the cactus forest – whether by accident or sub-conscious design I will never know. What I do know is that after walking for about twenty-five minutes without entering the forest, I knew I was lost. I tried to find some landmarks but the road I was on was descending and the bushes and trees blotted out the horizon. At no time was I frightened however because I knew I had only to retrace my steps and I'd be home. In a little while a truck came from the direction I was heading. This was the first sign of any life except for ground lizards, that I had seen for about a half hour.

I hailed the driver and asked, 'Bo ta papia Ingles?'

No, he didn't speak English.

'Spanish?'

Yes, a little.

'Estoy perdido!' (I'm lost,' in Spanish) then, 'Unda ta Sabana, aki of ei?' ('Where is Savana, here or there?' in Papiamentu).

He was a fine-looking young man with a little boy and he was at once concerned over my situation. He pointed in the opposite direction from the one I was taking and motioned to me to get in and said he would take me. I was so grateful that I had learned a little Spanish and enough Papiamentu to extricate myself from my error. It was difficult to make him understand just where I wanted to go but we finally pulled up in front of Mrs Pieters' house. I visited with her and the Reed family for a couple of hours, then got a ride home with a nice young Jamaican. He lives in Antriol and had brought Mr Reed home from work. Mr Reed had told this young Mr Sweebie that I was a 'missionary lady' and on the way home he asked me what my Faith was. We had a short but deep discussion and now not only does Mr Sweebie want to come again and talk to me about the Faith at greater length but he is going to bring me some wood to build a bookcase in the living room. He had heard of the Bahá'í Faith in Jamaica but it had only registered vaguely.

While I was at Mrs Pieters' I made several phone calls to men whose names Mr Mázgání had given me. While he was here, the week before I arrived, he had made several contacts. The people whose names he had given me were reporters – but he wasn't able to tell me for what. There is no local newspaper. I also called a man who had called Curaçao in response to a television program about the Faith. He wants to know more and was impressed and surprised to learn that there were Bahá'ís in the States. He said that only this week he had remarked to his children that he wished there was someone here who could tell him about the Bahá'í Faith. Things are looking up and I'm beginning to feel not so useless. Now we will have to see what problem the language barrier will be and how it will be resolved, because resolved it must be. There is no way that I can have real competence in Papiamentu or Spanish – and Dutch is out of the question. Bahá'u'lláh will really have to assist me if I am to be effective here at all.

July 6
7:30 p.m.

I'M so happy tonight! Mr Sweebie just left. He was here for almost four hours talking about the Faith! It was a completely satisfactory 'fireside'. His English is, of course, very good. He is an avid reader and has read a great deal about religion. His questions were penetrating and reasonable. He was baptized a Catholic but has had difficulty accepting much of the doctrine of Catholicism. He has been troubled by the number of faiths and the antagonism among them. He said he had hoped and prayed that there was a better way. He readily accepted the logic of the Faith and was so grateful for new insights into things that have been puzzling and troublesome. I had very little to give him to read and wished I had taken more literature with me. I have a fair supply of Papiamentu, some Spanish and Dutch, but hardly anything I want to part with in English. He says that at least three fellows who work with him – all Jamaicans – are also interested in knowing more about the Faith. Evidently he has been talking since I saw him yesterday. I gave him a couple of pamphlets for them and he feels sure they will want to come with him some evening to talk with me. I'm sure it doesn't really matter whom I teach but it is ironic that my first students are not Bonairians. Anyway, my little house has been blessed with its first fireside.

I was just interrupted by a young man – a boy, really, who wants to clean the front yard. It is terribly overgrown with weeds and brush. I hesitated to put up a 'Cas di Le Fe Bahá'í' because it looked so bad but I knew I wouldn't tackle it myself. He said at first that he would do it for 50 guilders and I just laughed at that. 50 guilders are about US$27.00! He began dealing on a descending scale, much to my amusement. He was such a nice boy, trying so hard to speak English – and he did a fairly good job – that when he reached 10 guilders, about US$5.35, I agreed to let him do it. It will be a hot, dirty job and well worth the money to get the place spruced up. I hope this cannot be considered an extravagance. He has a lovely name – Rutzel Castillio. He'll come tomorrow and when Rhoda gets back she won't know her place. Once the hard work is done I think if I give him a guilder or two every week he'll keep it up.

July 7
9:30 a.m.

MY two young men, the little Reed boys, have just come to get me. We will walk to town together. First we will pick up their mama. I can hardly wait to get to the post office. I feel, in my bones, there will be mail.

Later: Was there ever! I hit the jackpot!

July 8
10:00 a.m.

THE hot weather has begun. Already the water as it comes from the faucet is hot. The water for the houses is drawn off large storage tanks by pipes that lie above the surface of the ground. Normally the sun doesn't heat the pipes sufficiently for the water to get hot until about 2:00 p.m. so this should give you some idea of the heat pouring down at this early hour. Still, it is not really uncomfortable or unbearable. The blessed wind blows constantly but not with anger nor with force. It stirs up no dust, makes no demands. It caresses and soothes and makes everything bearable because it seems to care. However, one must learn to adjust life to the conditions. I am learning that the first thing I must do when I awake is to fill a water bottle for the refrigerator or I'd have to drink hot tea or coffee all day – or, ugh, soda pop! I do keep it on hand for my guests who drink the stuff like the Persians do. I have also learned that during these two months at least, July and August – and possibly September – a siesta in the afternoon is really helpful. Stores and businesses close down tight at the stroke of 12:00 noon. In less time than it takes to write it the streets are emptied of people and a hush falls over the island. Yesterday, because we got such a late start getting to town – Mrs Reed was unable to leave when the boys and I arrived – we were caught with our shopping not completed at noon and had to leave town. Everything is closed until 2:00 p.m. and then, as if by a kiss from a fairy tale prince, life instantly begins again.

Yesterday, again, I had the chance to prove myself and I wish I could feel proud but it turned out to be only a small victory after all. The boys and I walked to their home through the cactus forest and, with two small ones, one does not show fear – and really, with two laughing, running, playful boys there is no thought of fear. I determined that on my way home when I would be alone, I would brave the cactus forest! Again, as is almost always the case, the anticipation was more fearsome than the act itself. I WAS NOT AFRAID! I didn't have to pretend not to be afraid – I simply was not afraid! (Oh Tommy, my love, who has known me with fears no one else suspected, can you believe this?) Let some unbeliever tell me that prayers do not strengthen and support and change. Let someone without faith tell me that I, fear-ridden but forced by excessive pride to hide it from the world – save Tom – could live alone and sleep like a baby, safe and secure. For only one unfamiliar with the power of prayer would doubt it. Yet the miracles wrought through prayer are so personal, so unique, that one can hardly tell of them. Enough for me to say that I prayed for strength to stand against my fears only to discover that what I thought to be fearful is not so fearful at all. For me, this is miracle enough.

July 9
3:00 p.m.

YESTERDAY was rather a boring day. I more than half expected a visitor, a reporter – one of the men whose names Mr Mázgání had given me. I had phoned him and he was to come to see me. He suggested that perhaps an interview for the paper would be helpful and I readily agreed. I waited until about 3:00 p.m. and was so tired of sitting and reading that I decided to go for a walk. I didn't know or care where. As it turned out, I walked to town a new way and found it very pleasant and not too long. It took about 20 minutes of brisk walking. I had left a message on the front door inviting him to go in and wait. I got home about 4:40 and he had evidently not come. I remember saying many times that if one had any internal resources one would never be bored or lonesome. I still feel that is true. There has been enough in my life and enough to look forward to in the future that I am never bored. I'm never really lonesome. It's just that dad-blasted sitting that gets me down.

Today started out beautifully. It has been a day filled with children. About 9:00 a.m. my two little boys came and announced that they had come to spend the day with me. I suspect that they came to spend a part of the day with this typewriter – they are fascinated by it. Shortly after they arrived we were treated to another downpour of rain. To keep the boys amused until it stopped I let them type and was horrified to discover that the younger one, 11 years old, cannot spell the simplest words and can hardly read. The older, aged 12, who is really a very bright boy, does only a little better. He reads very well but cannot spell. For instance, 'are' becomes 'or', 'sister' is 'sustur', 'brother' is 'bruter'. When I think of my seven-year-old granddaughter and her proficiency in language I ache for these two children. Neville, the older, is really quick and learns fast. He has a good memory. We have been studying Papiamentu together and he can keep pace with me. I can only conclude that there must be something very wrong with the education system in Jamaica. (Of course, one must question the system under which I was educated – by the awful English in these letters. I take refuge, though, in the excuse that it's the machine and not me!)

After the sun came out again we started out for town. I had some wonderful mail in the box which made me very happy. We had to rush to the supermarket because it was nearing noon and the 'pumpkin' hour and I had to get more cat food. I made the discovery that I was not only feeding my two cats but all the cats in the area AND THE LIZARDS! It was my custom to set out a dish of food for the cats in the morning and then again in the evening. A dish of water is always outside for them. One morning I looked out and was horrified to see about a dozen lizards happily perched in and around the cats' feeding dish enjoying a gourmet breakfast. My kitties were nowhere in sight. I also found that chow call for my cats brought several other cats so now I don't put the food out until they ask for it. Then I practically stand out there with a shotgun to keep the moochers away! No wonder my poor little kitties stayed skinny. The baby kitty is beginning to know me and to trust me. It no longer runs away at my step but isn't yet brave enough to let me stroke it like the mama kitty does.

I fed the boys lunch and they played for awhile and went home. I had some washing to do so I wasn't displeased. I wish you could see my wash day here! I have a big old tin wash tub. I wait till afternoon when the water is really hot, use lots of washing soap and rubber gloves. I put my stuff in to soak, rubbing whatever stains there may be and leaving it to stay overnight. The next day, again in the afternoon, I rinse in several waters.

The water here is magic! I brought an old pair of white slacks with me that were badly stained. I had washed, pre-washed and bleached them at home and couldn't get the stains out. Why I packed them I really can't say except that I may have felt that if I had to do any dirty work they would come in handy. The first time I washed them here I could hardly believe what I was seeing. I hadn't even bothered to rub them because I felt, 'Oh, what's the use?' so you can imagine how I felt to see them sparkling white and clean – NO SPOTS!! I tell you the water is magic. But the sight of me sitting on the floor of the shower, washing out of a tub, should really be worth seeing. I hang the clothes out on a line in the back yard AFTER I chase the lizards away. The sun is so hot and good it bleaches white whiter than I have ever known it. The wind blows all the wrinkles out. All this and Heaven too!

This afternoon after all my work was done and I was again sitting and reading, a little girl walked slowly by – carrying a baby. I had seen her pass many times and had always waved and smiled at her, as I do to anyone who passes. Always before she had shyly turned away but today she returned my wave and waved the baby's hand. I motioned to her to come over to my gate and she did. As if this were a signal, about six other children appeared. I invited them in and, although they couldn't speak or understand one word of English and my Papiamentu is still so shaky, we got along fine. I learned their names and they mine. I gave them each a 'dushi' (a sweet). We laughed at each other and they left.

The oldest boy, a handsome little devil with black curly hair – indeed it was a mass of black ringlets that would have graced a Greek temple boy – black eyes full of laughter and mischief, a smile to melt the heart of a silly old grandmother, perhaps nine years old, had an ugly-looking machete in a plastic shopping bag. When I asked what it was for he tried to tell me and all I could make of it was that he was on his way to chop something down. It was a mean-looking knife, almost as tall as he was.

The children admired my house and asked about some of the things I have on my walls. I explained best as I could and they seemed satisfied. I think they were just glad that their questions were respected and answered. They left after a little while with promises to stop by again.

This was sooner than I had expected! In about half an hour my handsome machete boy called to me from the gate and asked permission to come in. His shopping bag was full and he pulled out a piece of something green, about eight inches long and about two inches around. The bag was full of like pieces. He made me understand that this was sugar cane and that was what his machete was for. I think he would have given me a piece if I had asked but I couldn't find out what to do with it. I learned later that they simply chew on it, extracting the sugar and spitting out the coarse stringy pulp.

The children have been by several times and, although they are all very dear, there are two I favor especially – the little machete boy and a little girl of about seven with skin like light milk chocolate, eyes like pools at midnight, lit by moonlight. Two of her front teeth are missing and her little pink tongue catches there when she talks. She is utterly adorable. These two have crept into my heart and I wish there was some way of being with them without the other children. I haven't yet found a way that won't hurt the others and I'm hoping that they will lose interest in me after awhile. I don't think those two will.

I'm becoming increasingly annoyed with my inactivity. I tell myself that it is lack of funds that prevents me from searching out those whose names I have. There is no such thing as an address here. You either know where someone lives or you know someone who does – or you just don't get there. Telephoning has been unsatisfactory. Today I put aside my excuse and made the decision that if they don't come to me I'll have to go to them. I have made arrangements with a taxi man who will come for me on Mondays, Wednesdays and Fridays and help me find people. He knows his way around and knows almost everyone on the island. I'm not going to waste another of these precious days. Money be hanged. I'll manage!

July 11
6:30 p.m.

I'M sitting on the porch of my little house. I think of it

as '*Mi kleine cas*'. Darkness is settling over the island. I'm facing east and I can see it come. I'm intrigued by the sounds that surround me. Here on the dirt road, about half a block from the main road called Papa Cornesweg, the sounds of traffic reach me very clearly and loudly. The auto-mechanic who lives in front of me is tuning up an old car and the grind and whirr of the ancient engine rides above the traffic noises. There are two little children in his house and I can hear small cries and much scolding. The words I don't recognize but the tone I do. Also, in front of me and across the road, they have turned up the radio and it blares and screams. I wish now that I had left part of my clothes at home and brought instead a tape recorder so that I could be free of the awful radio programs we get here. I've concluded – I hope not too hastily – that all contemporary, popular music in Spanish is rot. It is either sickeningly sweet or loud and crass. There are about six songs on the Spanish Hit Parade – oh yes, they have that too – that are called 'Corazón' – just that: 'Heart' – and each one is different. My ears long for some good music. Once in awhile – and never at the same place on the dial – I catch part of a movement of a symphony and once I heard about ten minutes of an absolutely divine string ensemble. Isn't it strange that with all the things I can do without the biggest deprivation seems to be music? Thank God for all the books I have access to.

I'm still on the porch, listening to night sounds. I can see the lights shining through the tin pieces of the house next door. There are many little children and the mother is 'big' again. The sounds from there are of hammer and saw. It seems that an addition is being built. The house already sprawls in every direction. I can't see where the addition will be. From the house of Papa Diek behind come the most annoying human sounds! They all have harsh, grating voices with only one way to use them – shouting. I haven't figured out yet if they are screaming at each other in anger or fun. I look for casualties each day but arms and heads seem intact so I'm beginning to believe that screaming is their normal way of communicating.

From all directions come the howling of dogs and the crowing of roosters. Over all is the sweet sound of the wind playing with the trees. It is constant but not insistent. It doesn't demand anything – not even attention – for the birds ignore it and continue to perch on the slim tree branches and contribute their sounds.

There is much variety among the birds. They are so beautiful and colorful. It's like having my very own aviary full of rare and exotic birds. I haven't any idea what they are. I had never before paid any attention to such things but, sitting here with nothing to do except listen and observe, my senses seem to be sharpening. I see a tiny little bird about the size of the first joint of my thumb. It has a long beak, is black with a yellow and/or yellow-red breast. It doesn't just fly – it hovers. There is also a little blue bird with a yellow breast and there are green birds. I saw two that looked like tiny parrots. I knew they weren't parakeets. They were much larger and their beaks were long, hooked and sharp. They cavorted like love-birds and I've only seen them in pairs. Whatever size, shape and color birds come in, I'm sure I see them. I know there is no nightingale among them for I haven't heard a sweet sound out of them – just chirping and yipping and scolding. Yet it is not unpleasant. The sweetest sound is the sound of the wind

. . . I've said that so often. It is to me the one most outstanding feature of this island and I'm sure it wasn't intended that any other sounds compete with it. It gentles all the harshness of this barren rocky soil and encases in its velvet all other sounds.

All this I wrote while the island was being wrapped in darkness. When it was too dark to see what I was writing I came in and typed it. I'll read for awhile and go to bed. I'm terribly disappointed about not being able to find a single reading lamp on the island. I've written to the friends in Curaçao and asked them to try to find one for me there and send it on the ferry. I know my eyes won't hold out much longer and if I can't read and can't listen to good music and have no one to talk to then this will for me be my most great prison. Maybe this is the testing that I need. If it is, I had better learn how to handle it.

I've given myself a satisfying job. I don't remember if I mentioned it yet. I am compiling an English to Papiamentu dictionary. Using the one language book that is available, but which is without a dictionary section, I am reviewing each page through the alphabet and listing in true order all English words and their Papiamentu counterparts. It will be a very limited thing because Mr Groili, the author, uses very simple language but it could be a valuable supplement to his book. As soon as I have it halfway done I will write him and offer it to him. All the words in his book will be included and a few others that he doesn't use, like broom, mop, sink, faucet, lamp, etc. I am doing at least one letter of the alphabet each day which means that, in less than a month, it should be finished. It is the kind of detailed, demanding work that I love and doesn't tax my eyes too much. If I don't do another thing for the Faith here I feel that this will be a service to those pioneers who surely will follow Rhoda and me. Rhoda hasn't bothered to learn Papiamentu. She relies on her Spanish which, I understand, is pretty good.

Papiamentu is to spoken language what shorthand is to writing. If there is a shorter way to say something, these people have found it. For instance – 'Con ta bai?' is literally 'How is it going?' but is used instead of 'Hello' or 'How are you?' and is shortened to 'Con bai?' and even to 'Bai?'. 'I don't know' is 'Mi na ta sa' and is shortened to 'Mi n' sa.' And so it goes in Papiamentu. The word itself means 'that which is spoken'. It was never intended to be a written language. Even the spelling has been simplified. In Spanish it is 'verde' for green but pronounced 'berde' which is exactly what it is in Papiamentu. Water in Spanish is 'aqua', pronounced 'awa', which is exactly what it is in Papiamentu. It is the simplest language in the world, certainly not the richest. With steady application it could be learned in three months. I hope I haven't bored you with this.

July 20
10:00 a.m.

It has been ten days since I have written anything. When last I wrote, on a Friday, I knew I was going to the beach on that Sunday and I wanted to wait so that I could record, as accurately as possible, what it was like. The day at the beach was indeed a delight. Actually I spent four hours there in the company of Poppy, a sister of Raphael. I shall probably tell more about those four hours later. If I had written about it at that time, I would have filled page after page with ecstatic, and probably bad, prose.

As it turned out, I spent from the following Monday until today in a condition of hell – or something very close to it – that I hope not to experience again. During the week before my 'beach' day, I had been aware of 'something' irritating on my back – just below the left shoulder blade and a little to the right of it. I thought it was a bite, mosquito or spider, and I treated it with what salves and unguents I had with me. It continued to annoy and itch until Monday when it became downright ugly and pained so much that sleep was impossible. Tuesday morning I knew I had to see the doctor – in spite of the stories I had heard about him. It was said that inasmuch as he was not only a doctor for people but also a veterinarian, he treated all his patients like animals; that he was unfeeling, rough, preferred animals to people and other calumnies of that kind.

The truth, I discovered, was far different. Dr Welvaart, a big, handsome and very blond Dutchman of about forty, was very gentle, very courteous and very concerned. He explained that I had a very large cyst that had gone into secondary infection. I still don't know what that actually means! He explained that the pus would have to be drawn out by the application of salves, that it would be painful and take time and that, in the end, he would probably have to cut.

The first thing he did was to make an incision and this he did without any warning or preparation – no nice sedative or pain-killer – just a quick slice with the knife – and I was ready to die! At least, for one quick second, I wished I had. He did a lot of scraping and cleaning and then applied a drawing salve. He gave me two prescriptions, one for pain and one for fever (which was already very high) and told me to return in two days.

All the time he worked on me I had my fist jammed into my mouth to keep from screaming. I almost laughed, and it would have been hysterically had I managed it, because I thought of the silver bullet bit from the old Western movies where the kind old village doctor is removing a bullet from the hero's back and a faithful side-kick and buddy says, 'Here, Kid, try this silver bullet. It'll help a heap.' Of course the part of the scenario I had to leave out was the part where they pour half a bottle of rot-gut down his throat. Now, after chewing through my knuckles, I was sure it was the bottle rather than the silver bullet that did the job. However the thought did tickle me and kept me from going through the ceiling.

I wish I could say that was the worst of it. I know that I walked to the doctor's office on Tuesday – I haven't any idea how I got home! The office is at one end of town and their shopping area, where I would normally get a taxi, is at the other end. Somehow I got home. The fever had intensified to the point where I was screamingly hot one minute then shivering with cold the next. I had just enough sense to remember to take the medicine and I think that was only because I knew it would bring some oblivion in sleep. I was to return in two days and when I was about to leave the house the two little Reed boys arrived. It was strange that for two days no one had come by. Usually Carlos and sometimes Loie Martis, my near neighbor, would drop by – but not on these two days when I would have so welcomed anyone.

3:30 p.m.

THE drugs the doctor gave me had begun to take hold and I became too muddle-headed to continue – so I've been sleeping until a little while ago. Now, as a relief from utter boredom, I'll try this again. I hope it comes out sense! When I went to the doctor the first time, I went early in the morning – about 8:45 – and already there were 36 ahead of me. I know that because each is given a little wooden token with a number. Each number is consecutively given. Mine was 'trente shete' or 37 – very elementary. I waited about two and a half hours to see the doctor and, in that time, realized that the morning hours were for patients he treated under government regulations. I don't yet understand the system but it is a kind of socialized medicine, although different from what we understand by the term. When I think more clearly I'll find out more about how it works.

After the doctor had done his first bit of probing and I was ready to leave, I asked about paying and he told me not to worry about it.

'When we have made you well, you will pay.'

He made the next appointment for the second day, Thursday. I don't want to think about Tuesday and Wednesday. If I had tried to write this during that time the paper would have dripped with self-pity and weakness. I felt so alone; couldn't have eaten if food had been offered to me, but it would have felt so good to have screamed, 'Go away and don't bother me!' at someone. Isn't that perverse? I shivered and I pained and I sobbed and if that isn't a wasted performance without an audience I don't know what is! In my greatest hour, to be on stage in an empty theatre. What irony!

The drawing salve was indeed drawing and, at times, it felt as if it were drawing me out of myself. I had arranged for a taxi to fetch me Thursday afternoon and this time the doctor really out-did himself and me too. I was trembling with fear before I got on the table and had my 'silver bullet' fist ready for my mouth, but I was in no way ready for what I felt! For about five minutes I whimpered and sobbed and 'Oh, Doctor-ed' while he dug and probed and expressed. I felt thoroughly ashamed and begged his pardon, perhaps too profusely.

Sweet man that he is, he put his hand on my shoulder and salvaged my pride and restored a shred of dignity when he said, 'Dear lady, I know how painful that is. I have done just that to men who have screamed and fainted. You have been very brave.'

Because his office is closed at the weekend he told me to go to the hospital Saturday to have the dressing changed. The hospital is a private one that seems to be part of the Catholic church but isn't. It's called Sint Franciscu Hospital and is adjacent to the church but I am told it is not affiliated. It is staffed only by nurses and nurses' aides or trainees who are called 'sisters'. The doctor – and there are only two on the island – comes in for emergencies or for a private patient. I'm going to dig into this a little further too. Two doctors on an island of 9000 people sounds a little incredible.

The nurse who changed the dressing was an angel. She was so gentle and so tender. She said it would be better if the dressing were changed two or three times a day but since that is not possible if I were to come again on Sunday it would help. She also suggested that I keep wet compresses over the dressing. It is impossible to say what a change from pain that has brought. It is a little difficult to manage but not impossible and the results are so satisfying that the effort is worth it.

It had been so strange that with the exception of Loie Martis, who feels just as helpless in the face of sickness as Tom does, no one else came by. If Raphael had come I'm sure he would have had his mother or sister come in to help me. Taxis don't work on Sunday and I wondered how I would get to the hospital but good old

Loie came through and got someone to take me and bring me back. The worst is still to come. Tomorrow I go to the doctor again and, if the swelling and fever have gone down sufficiently, he will cut out the cyst. I don't expect any anaesthesia and all I can hope is that it will be quick and that I behave decently. It is interesting to note that I have lost 14 pounds (or six-plus kilos) and if I can manage to keep them off maybe I'll reckon the whole experience worthwhile – after awhile, a good, long while!

One of my constant worries has been the cats. I ran out of cat food days ago and have not been near a store to buy any. Fortunately I had some dry kibble kind of stuff which they don't care for but once a day I manage to pull myself out back and set out a dish for them and replenish their water. They know something is wrong, at least the mama cat does. She lies out near the back door – something she has not done before. They don't like the food but when I beg them to eat it they oblige. They are so sweet.

July 24
10:30 a.m.

I FEEL really good today. I'm sorry now that I began this account while I was not sure where I was heading. I'll try to fill in the blanks.

I went to the doctor on the 21st and all he did was change the dressing – plus a little squeezing for good measure – so I wouldn't get too cocky, I guess. But it wasn't too bad. I was to return on Wednesday. That suited me fine because I couldn't convince myself that what I wanted most for my birthday (which was

Tuesday) was a sharp scalpel in the back! Tuesday was a nice day. I was feeling a little sad and forlorn – but not excessively so – and when the little Reed boys arrived early in the morning I sent them for a taxi and went with them to their new house.

The Reeds have moved from Mrs Pieters' where they were never too happy. They were cramped into two very small sleeping rooms there and there was always the problem of two 'porky' women sharing the same small kitchen. As soon as Mrs Reed was able she found a house and moved into it. That was one of the reasons I hadn't seen her or the boys during those days when I was so bad.

Mrs Reed was very dear and insisted that I eat something. She had become aware of my food peculiarities and didn't even offer me the goat stew she was fixing for their lunch. She did fix a hamburger patty (out of fresh ground steak) and a little rice and red beans but she agonized over the smallness of the amount I would accept. You simply wouldn't believe the size of the platters of food she consumes, complaining all the while how she can't lose weight. She is a dear sweet woman and I shall always love her.

After I had eaten – and I must admit it was the first cooked, solid food I'd had in days – I chewed it very carefully and slowly because I wanted it to stay down and I wanted to please that dear lady – she made me lie down. That had become my pattern: up for awhile, on my back for awhile.

I slept for an hour and awoke to the sound of an American voice. It was one of the ladies from the Trans World Radio Church. The church had been helpful in getting the Reeds moved in and had found some needed furniture for them. Those people are really wonderful and someday I'll do a paper just on them. Joan had come to invite the boys to her little girl's birthday party on Wednesday and to take home a pot of the goat stew Mrs Reed had fixed for them. We visited for awhile and Mrs Reed asked her if she could come back later and drive me home. She could, she would and she did. Of course in the meantime we made a big thing out of the two birthdays and Margo and I wished each other 'Happy Birthday'. Later that afternoon Joan's car pulled up outside, Mrs Reed got out carrying a little plate and presented me with two frosted cupcakes, each with a candle. Joan had made them while she was making Margo's birthday cake. I'm sure there is no need to tell how I felt. There is so much goodness in the people and of all the goodness in the world, that which comes from people is the most sweet.

Early that evening Raphael came by. He had just changed jobs and had been busy working long shifts while he was familiarizing himself with the post. He will be managing the office at the Flamingo Beach Club, the second largest resort hotel on the island. He says it is a demanding job and he had to work all shifts so that he could understand the needs of each. He was very sorry to learn I had been ill and suggested I might like to go for a drive. It was still early and much daylight remained. It was an exciting drive. It is hard to believe that on so small an island there can be so much variety and so much to see. We drove till quite late then came home and had lemonade and my two birthday cupcakes. It has been a really nice day after all. When I show my slides and pictures I'll be better able to explain so much more I don't feel up to writing about at this time.

I have just written to the Regional Teaching Committee in Curaçao though, as follows:

Dear Friends,

Please accept this first official report from Bonaire. Unfortunately there are no victories or successes to report. I have tried unsuccessfully to make contact with those whose names Mr Mázgání gave me. I have spoken to the gentlemen on the phone and, in most cases, each promised to call on me but I have seen no one. For the past ten days I have been very ill. A cyst or an abscess developed on my back which was so painful and caused such high fever that I was in bed for about four days. Since there is no one near who could know that I was sick, I was alone and very miserable. Now I am much better and although I must still go to the doctor to have fresh dressings put on, I am at least without pain and fever. I shall try to resume making contacts in a day or so.

Everyone here seems to be aware of the name 'Bahá'í'; everyone to whom I have spoken takes it for granted that there should be a Bahá'í here. I have found a lot of indifference and apathy but no resentment. People have been so kind. I love the Bonairians and I have fallen in love with Bonaire itself. I am learning its history, its customs and its language. I know its geography as if it were my own land. I have found nothing negative here but it may be that I need guidance and that I am missing something. I ask for such guidance.

Devotedly, in His service,

Marion West

I had hoped to find the energy to walk to town this morning but couldn't quite push myself that far. At the moment I'm glad I didn't because after writing several letters and this account, it is well past 12:00 noon and I shall stop for prayers and siesta. How gratefully I have learned to accept siesta.

July 25

I DID walk to town this afternoon. I knew that if ever I were to get some strength back I had better start pushing. I managed the walk in great shape, went to the bank, the post office, did a little bit of shopping and tried to find a taxi. After waiting what seemed forever I gave it up as a lost cause and determined somehow to make it home '*na pi'a*' (on foot). I hadn't gone more than a couple of blocks before I realized that, no matter how convincingly I tried to say, 'It just takes putting one foot before the other', I couldn't possibly make it, was almost prepared to sit down in the road and cry – when along came a taxi. He had no right to be there, as I learned, because all taxis come in off the road and go to the airport at that time of day; it was absolutely a fluke that he was on his way there so late. He detoured, though, and took me home. I guess the name of the game is, 'How much can Marion take?'

The whole Reed family – this included Papa Reed – walked over to visit me last night. It was a wonderful and welcome surprise. They stayed for about an hour and helped me pass another night that would have been lack-lustre and dull without them.

In the next installment I'll try to fill in what I see are big gaps.

July 29

THE wind from the east is honey and silk; sometimes it seems like a kitten's paws with the tiny claws just barely discernible. It's the east wind that wraps the island in its soft but relentless embrace, but it is good and one feels secure in its envelopment. The west wind is indeed the Wicked Witch of the West! It rarely troubles the island and it is said that it has been many years since it bothered Bonaire with its awful presence. But one day 'IT' came and it was evil and destructive!

I was sitting at the typewriter feeling a little rocky – not quite recovered from high fever and much pain – when I became aware of a rocking, pounding battering at my back door which faces west. It was a strange sound but I was sure I hadn't heard all the sounds of Bonaire and didn't pay too much attention. But attention 'IT' wanted and, to get it, 'IT' tore at the house with great fury!

At the back of the house – where the afternoon sun pours in – there is a sunshade. You've seen them: they are made of narrow strips of wood and roll up or down on cords. They are usually hung outside. This one was quite large. It covered the entire window of the back room (my storage room) and was very securely fastened to the roof of the house with heavy iron hooks and chains at the top. At the bottom it hung loose. It had become a favorite resting place for my kitties. They climb on top of the boxes and lumber stored under the window and behind the sunshade. The sky had darkened but not heavily. It was as if that evil wind was saying, 'See, I can do my dirty work in the light. I don't have to hide behind the darkness!' It howled and screamed around the house and I fully expected to see the small trees and shrubs out back pulled up by the roots. Because they are so small and insignificant I think it didn't bother with them. It had bigger things in mind, as I later discovered.

I was trying to ignore the fury when suddenly, with a wrench and a grind, the sunshade was ripped off and thrown against the dining-room glass door where I had been sitting. Now that shade must have been expensive. It was one that Rhoda had put up and I knew that, unless I did something, it wouldn't even be good for kindling. I went outside and with whatever I could find – rocks, boards, boulders – I anchored it down. So many funny thoughts came to my mind. I thought of the deck of a ship in a storm – at least, the movie storms – and could see the ropes strung out on deck to give the crew something to hold onto while they did their chores – and wished I had such ropes. I knew I was going to be lifted up like Dorothy and carried to 'No Such Land'! I was never so glad for those extra pounds I have always hated; perhaps they held me down!

When I got back into the house I started to laugh because another thing came to mind. I doubt any of you will remember this but when I was a little girl there was a funny record that we loved at our house. It was the Bill Cosby monologue of its day. It was called 'Cohen on the Telephone' and was so funny that even now when I can barely remember it I must still laugh over it. Mr Cohen makes his call – there are many different scripts but the funniest is where he begins, 'Last night der came alung a vint and it blew down mine shut-ters.' From there he proceeds to list all the terrible things that happened to him but he makes it sound so funny. He makes such fun of himself (it is so typically and deliciously Jewish) that you are howling with laughter. Well, 'Cohen on the Telephone' came to my mind as I sat there recovering from my tussle with the west wind. It was some time before I could compose myself. There is something a little self-conscious making about laughing alone. Why should that be? Why does laughter have to be shared while tears beg for solitude? But I sat laughing till the tears came. I thought, well, now I can say, 'There came a vint and it blew down mine shut-ter!'

The worst of the storm was what it did to the shoreline. Fortunately, there had been coastguard warnings and most of the fishing boats and pleasure craft were able to be brought into small and sheltered coves but one of the piers was literally ripped out of the water and tossed up on the beach. The wind lashed with such fury at the beaches that it stripped away the sand entirely and left only the rocky coral bottom exposed. When I had gone to the beach at the Hotel Bonaire before it had the finest, whitest, smoothest beach that could be found anywhere. When I went yesterday it looked like a nightmare. As you approached the water's edge, instead of sand you found only rock and you understood what is meant by a coral reef. I spoke to Captain Don Stewart and he said it will cost the hotel thousands of dollars to find sand, dredge it up and lay it down on their beach. First they will have to lay a bed of small stones, shells and bits of coral; if they don't the sand will just wash away. He was sick about it. He said the beach of the Hotel Bonaire was man-made to start with. There are only a few natural beaches on the island and they are so far away from everything as to make them impractical for commercial use. I understand the government has given permits for two more hotels to be built on Bonaire – but no more, thank God. The best way to kill this lovely place would be to commercialize it.

Capt Don is a local character, an American who runs the scuba and aqualung department and store. He teaches all that fancy underwater stuff, has a large and competent staff of guides and teachers, organizes underwater exploration parties, and is much loved, respected and feared. He is a big man – very handsome although his body and face carry many scars. He wears little wire earrings, has a voice that even on land sounds as if it were under water, and is a thoroughly engaging and fascinating man. He and his wife are friends of Rhoda's and he welcomed me warmly. When he first heard that I was Rhoda's replacement on Bonaire, he simply said, 'Well, I wish you luck.'

While I was at the beach yesterday I met a group of Americans from Ohio who had come on a scuba vacation. They were delightful people in their late twenties or early thirties, not kids, who had heard that the best underwater sport in the world can be found at Bonaire. It seems that there are travel agencies that promote vacations of that sort. They have all fallen in love with Bonaire and I expect that many will return. I have found that there are many expatriates from the States living their retirement years here.

July 31

I HAD a delightful surprise yesterday. A packet of messages from many of the friends at Clear Creek Bahá'í School arrived in the mail and kept me reading for about an hour. So many expressions of love and encouragement: I doubt if the friends can ever understand what those notes meant to me. I wish I could answer every one of them . . . I'll try but it gets rather expensive. I found out that post cards, even if sent airmail, take about one month to be delivered. Those marvelous little aerogrammes often reach their destinations in five days, rarely longer than ten days. I understand I'm getting a tape recorder AND tapes for my birthday (which was on the 22nd) from Tom and some others. I can hardly wait! Days I can manage easily; if all else fails there's always this typing to do but nights are rough. I think I know the time every northbound plane flys overhead after dark; I think I know the position of every star in the sky – although not its name or constellation; I think I can tell exactly when the moon will rise during certain quarters. The radio reception, while not so bad during the day, is impossible at night. There seem to be too many stations coming in on the same frequency. Tom would be saying at this point, 'Don't you wish you knew as much as you think you know about that?' and he'd be right. I don't know at all what jams everything up – all I do know is that it is impossible to get good reception. The tape recorder will be right out of heaven!

The doctor has almost discharged me. At least I don't have to have dressings changed every other day. This time I can go a whole week without seeing him – although I'll have to find someone to change the bandages every day. I don't need any more of that salve so anybody with a strong stomach can re-do the dressings. I think it needs a strong stomach because the doctor says there is a big hole there and MY stomach needs to be strong for that. I feel great. I'm able to walk both ways to and from the *playa*. My appetite is returning – which I'm going to have to watch. I'm not about to sacrifice that lovely weight loss.

I am anticipating a visit from a member of the Pioneer Teaching Committee early in August. He is an American, Don Newby from Salina, Kansas, who left the States to pioneer about four years ago. I haven't met him but he wrote to say we had many mutual friends and he knows of me. Also, I hope to spend the Feast of Asmá' with the Bahá'ís of Curaçao. I will try to arrange to fly over on Monday, the Feast is on Tuesday, then I would like to come back on the ferry. I saw the ferry and it's more like the Albany night boat or a Mississippi River excursion boat. They have several restaurants on board and dancing and entertainment. It sounds like fun and I'm sorry that I'll be enjoying it by myself. This is another one of those times when I feel the need of Tom so much. This is the kind of time when we should be together. He humors me in my almost childish delight with anything new or exciting. If I want to clap my hands and/or squeal that's all right with him; his enjoyment of my enjoyment makes the pleasure so much greater. Does that make sense? I know it will to him.

I wish I could say that I'm progressing faster than I am at Papiamentu – but the sad thing is that everyone wants to practice his English on me and is almost hurt if we spend too much time on Papiamentu. I find I am left with a vocabulary and no place to go with it. I'm still at it, though, and have a little eleven-year-old girl who comes in every day who doesn't speak one word of English. I manage to understand her about half of the time and succeed in getting her to understand me about the same. The language book, I have found, is not much use. Mr Goilo's Papiamentu is stiff and formal and not at all what the people speak.

Mrs Reed and I are planning another trip to the beach tomorrow. I am getting such a gorgeous, mellow tan. I would love to lie out there every day but that would be too much of a good thing. Going only two or three times a week makes it an excursion and we look forward to it. We pack a lunch and I take a book and the time passes beautifully.

August 1
2:00 p.m.

I'm learning a little better how to accept disappointments – not to qualify for 'radiant acquiescence' yet – but slowly getting there. Last night Mr Sweebie was to come for dinner and more Bahá'í talk. It was his idea to come for talk and mine that he come for dinner. He is a bachelor, lives alone and mostly eats out. I hate to cook for myself and often don't, so the opportunity of cooking for someone again was irresistible. I cooked a really good man-type meal, set the table and waited – and waited. Mr Sweebie didn't show up. I can only assume that, in the week since his last visit, he forgot or that a better prospect than spending the evening in the company of an old lady came up. I'm sure he will appear one day, embarrassed and ashamed. But in the meantime my disappointment was there.

Today, I had made firm arrangements with what I thought was a very dependable taxi man to pick me up at 11:00 a.m. and take me to the Reeds' where they would join me on our planned trip to the beach. I had walked to town for mail and to visit my dear friend Carlos Mercera who was so helpful when I first arrived here. He is now in hospital. I got back home at about 10:10. I had lunch packed, goodies for the two boys, my book, sun-tan lotion, towels and everything and, again, I waited – and waited – and no Nicholas (the taxi man)! I wasn't so upset for myself but neither the Reeds nor I have a phone and there was no way I could let them know that I hadn't goofed. Today is extremely hot and muggy and the beach would have been heavenly.

However, out of every poison we are told to distill honey and honey I had. Today in the mail my birthday present from family and friends arrived – a cassette tape recorder that is a beaut! It is simplicity itself – which means that even I can operate it. It has good tone and there was a prize package included – a Feast held in Sparks in which the entire community participated and all of whose voices I listened to like a child sucking a lollipop. I savored each voice, played parts back so that I could repeat the sweetness and, after I had played it over and over, I found myself licking my lips in gorgeous remembrance of those beloved voices. What can I say? The best remedy for loss of appetite is hunger!

I see that I haven't mentioned the misfortune that struck my poor, dear Carlos. He had been to see me on a Thursday afternoon and had complained again of pains in his legs, particularly in his knees. I tried to urge him to slow down, not to walk all over the island making his mercy calls. He laughed and said he was fine – just getting a little old. He's 86. Friday morning he had a stroke and all I could think was that it was a blessing that it hadn't happened at night on his way through the cactus forest where he would have lain (is that right?) until morning. I had learned about it on my way to the doctor's office Friday morning and hurried to Carlos' home to learn that he was being moved to the hospital. I've been to see him every day this week and ache for him.

His right side is paralyzed. He will never walk again and his family is not too keen on taking care of him. They are more than a little unforgiving that he gave up his Netherlands citizenship. He carries American papers. Because of that he is unable to get help here from the government and his Social Security, which I urged the family to investigate, evidently pays no benefits out of the country. I wish somebody at home could check that out. He worked in the States for more than 50 years and does have a Social Security card. He has a pretty good pension from, I think, a shipping line he worked for as a seaman but his family is afraid it won't be enough to keep him in a rest home. They have made it quite clear that they don't want him. In fairness to them I must say that he, Carlos, wanted to be independent of them, let them know he didn't think too highly of them so their reaction is not without some justification. He wanted to be free of them and they knew it. Now they would like to be free of him and I'm sure he knows it.

For a few days he lay in almost a coma; the last two days he has been more alert. Yesterday he knew me and I joked with him; he always liked a joke. He's the old man who said I had deceived him into thinking I spoke Papiamentu. He was so good to me. I had only to think of something that needed fixing or doing and he was there. He built a wonderful bookcase for me because I said how naked the living room looked without books. When I admired the bookcase and said that if there was a piece of that good heavy lumber left I would like it for a bread-cutting board, he showed up the next day with a dandy that he had made, sanded and polished. It even had a hole in it so that I could hang it up. He is so loved by everyone. I'm sure even his family loves him but familial sensitivities being what they are, the situation is not unusual. Every nurse and aide in the hospital knows at every minute what his condition is. Everyone can tell you if he ate well today, how he slept, and even more personal matters if they were inquired about. I know that God's Will will be done in any event but if I dare nudge the Divine Will just a little, it would be in the direction of not permitting a proud, loving, tender old man to be a burden to family and/or friends.

I'm on my way to town to buy some tapes. There is no way I can thank you enough, my dear friends, for this wonderful tape recorder. It will safeguard my sanity. I hope I can find a shop that has good classical recordings and then I won't care if a dozen Mr Sweebies don't show up. Now that's a little whistling in the dark because I do care. I'm not here just to listen to good or bad recordings, am I?

I have had promises from so many people that they would call on me. Some were those who were supposed to be interested in hearing more about the Faith. They would make firm appointments and not show up. That seems to be the way. So I sit and wait, too restless and eager to read or write – and time passes and I'm still sitting. How heavenly to sit and listen to things I want to hear. I'm hoping that Tom will be able to send me some of the good Bahá'í tapes that he knows I love and if I can't find good stuff here, I'll yell. O.K.?

I especially thank George for mailing the recorder. It arrived in prime condition on August 1 – today.

I know you all love me. I feel it pouring over and I love you all too. I know how difficult I have been at times and all I can say is that many of the traits that irritated you all are being purged out – the hard way. Because I want your love – and I have always wanted it – I think Bahá'u'lláh is teaching me how to be lovable. Again, God bless you all and my love and prayers are with you.

August 2
7:30 a.m.

THOUGHTS are coming so fast that I must get them down before they float back into that world of thoughts that brought them into being in the first place. Yesterday I bought some tapes for my newly-acquired treasure. Choosing was difficult because the shop had a marvelous collection of good music. I finally chose the Schubert 'Trout' quintet, Beethoven's 'Eroica', Bach's 'Brandenburg Concertos' and a medley of stuff like Beethoven's 'Egmont Overture', Bizet's 'L'Arlésienne Suite', some Handel, Chopin, Mozart, etc.

I got drunk last night on all that heavy wine and wallowed in it but came to the conclusion that my favorite is Bach. I am convinced that the music composed by Bach, and especially the 'Brandenburgs', is the most civilized in the world. For me its appeal lies in its precision, its order and the almost absolute justice of its arguments. For me, it reaches levels of awareness that are purely spiritual and it evokes patterns of such mathematical majesty that I feel drawn into a better place and am a better person for it. I am listening to it again as I type. Like the purity of Bonaire water and air, I can't seem to get my fill of it. I discover that while I may be lonely, I cannot ever be lonesome in the same sense that, even if I were poverty-striken, I would never be poor. Bach makes me take a good look around and see the very richness of the gift of life itself. I see a world decked out in such gorgeous array: gold and rose, greens of every hue. I hear all the marvelous sounds, even the sound of man. I look into the heart of the lovely plant growing just outside my door and feel it tremble at my touch and know that all life throbs with the gift of God and I feel richer than any king. I had a music teacher once who said that when I mastered five-finger exercises so that I could make them sound like music, I would be on my way to being a musician. Well, the truth is, I never did; I lacked the discipline necessary to perfect anything. But as I listen to the Brandenburgs I understand what she meant.

I'm absolutely and positively joyful this morning. Part of it is Bach; the other is a visit I had quite late last night. I was sitting out on the veranda enjoying everything. I won't attempt to separate the sounds and the smells and the sights of the late summer sky. Everything enchanted me. It was about 9:45 and I began to think that it might be time to start getting ready for bed when a car pulled up outside my gate.

A voice said, 'Mrs West, is that you? Do you remember me?'

In a flash, even before I saw his face, I knew this was Rigoberto Meléndrez, a young Curaçaon I had met in

Dr Rabbani's house. I had spent one evening with him and found him delightful, keenly intelligent, filled with high aspirations. He was both a TV personality and a teacher of languages. He taught Spanish, Dutch and Papiamentu and was anxious to perfect his English so he could teach that too. He had come to Bonaire as a reporter for the Miss Teen contest final being held here. It would decide who would be 'Miss Netherlands Antilles'.

Rigoberto had arrived late, by plane from Curaçao. There had been engine trouble on that little nothing of an airplane which I had flown in from Curaçao several weeks ago. The whole flight from Curaçao is only about fifteen minutes but it is entirely over water. Rigoberto said that about five minutes out one of the engines died and they had to return to Curaçao to wait until another plane was run out. When he arrived in Bonaire, with two other young men, they were told at the Hotel Bonaire that their accommodation had not been held for them and there was not a spare room on the island.

This inter-island contest is very important. People come from all the islands – and this includes St Maarten. It is to be marveled at that this tiny island, whose 9000 population must have quadrupled, didn't submerge under the added weight! Rigoberto, who didn't know just where I lived, inquired of the uncle of his friends – who had kindly offered the boys sleeping room – if he knew where I lived and of course he knew.

'Oh, the American lady in Antriol. Yes, I know.'

It was he who drove Rigoberto here at that late hour. Rigoberto had come on two accounts; first to let me know he was here and, although he has not made his formal declaration as a Bahá'í, he is on fire with the love of it. He wants to do anything he can to help me spread the Word. He would be happy to translate for me. Unfortunately he is to be here only until Monday, so we only have all day Sunday. Secondly, he asked me to be his guest at the Miss Teen contest. He had two tickets. I was delighted.

He was hungry. I fed him the dinner I had prepared for Mr Sweebie. It had been cooling its heels in the refrigerator.

August 3

I KNEW my beautiful Raphael was to be one of two masters-of-ceremonies at the Miss Teen contest and I wanted to see this extraordinary young man in action. Remember, Raphael is a young man – island born and raised. With the exception of a two-year hitch in the army, stationed in Aruba (another island), he has not been out of the country and yet he has the dignity of a young king. His command of languages, including English, and the power in his voice and the lordliness of his bearing make him a joy to behold. For my money, he makes other MCs look like country louts, coarse and common. He even brought a fineness to a very second-rate presentation which peddled sex in the usual way of all such contests.

The thing that made it difficult for me to watch the contest was the extreme youth of the girls; one was as young as fourteen. Almost without exception each knew well how to use her little underformed body to say, 'I may not have it yet but I know what it's for and I intend to use it. Buy my wares, buy my wares.' It was a little sickening. One sweet little thing, who was awarded the title 'Miss Amity', I named 'La Paloma'. She did indeed look like a little pigeon or dove with her rounding breasts pushed out before her and her little tush pushed out behind. She strutted in the way of a female dove, calling attention to herself before an admiring set of males. It was so cute, yet so silly.

Raphael gave to each contestant, as he introduced her, a higher station than the performance called for. He looked so handsome in his white suit, with the colors of the Netherlands Antilles in a long, wide band gracing the right side from shoulder to trouser cuff. The suit had what we call a Nehru collar and reminded me again of his exquisite taste in clothes. My feelings were entirely ambivalent at that point. On the one hand I thought, 'What a waste of quality. What could this boy do in the States?' On the other hand I thought, 'Oh God, protect this boy from the spoilage of a rotten society. Keep him fine and clean.'

Rigoberto and I had fun picking the three finalists, second guessing the judges. We were right on all three counts. There really wasn't too much choice, especially when you consider that while there were some very appealing and beautiful dark-skinned girls in the finals, all the judges but one were lily-white. I asked Rigoberto how a white judge could fairly judge the beauty of a dark-skinned girl. He or she would almost certainly judge by white standards and, of course, that's what happened. The girl chosen 'Miss Teen' was really very beautiful. She carried herself with grace and dignity, showed more than normal discipline and poise and was simply and tastefully gowned. I'm sure all these things impressed the judges.

Rigoberto and friends had called for me in a car, driven by the uncle who was to pick us up at midnight after the contest was over. In the crowded stadium we lost the two friends and never found them. I have never seen a stadium so packed, not even in TV shots of some of the most heavily attended games in the States. We had arrived late – as Rigoberto said, 'Curaçao time' – and we had to stand the whole while (three and a half hours!), pushed and stepped on, but able to secure a vantage spot where we could see and hear very well. We were so close to the stage that Raphael spotted us and waved.

Afterwards we tried to find the uncle's car and/or friends but finally gave up and decided to walk the short distance to town to try to find a taxi. I was all for walking home – not much farther than I usually walk every day – but Rigoberto wouldn't hear of it. He felt it would be dangerous and unsafe. That may be true in Curaçao, unfortunately, but I don't feel it is true here. Anyway, I would have felt safe but Rigoberto was firm. His intentions were great but we found that it was after midnight and every place where we might have phoned for a taxi – even if they had been running at that time – was closed down tight. The streets were full of laughing, dancing, singing, shouting young people. I wanted to run and shout with them except that while I KNOW how young I feel, I'm not always sure if others see it and my good sense, sometimes, keeps me from making a fool of myself. I was very tired in spite of my high feelings and told Rigoberto that I was simply going to sit down on a store-front stoop and wait for something to happen. He, poor darling, was very unhappy and blamed himself. Alone, he could have gone up to any bunch of fellows and begged a ride to his host's house but he was afraid for me.

My mother used to tell me that I didn't have enough sense to be afraid of people and I guess she may have been right but I know that this lack of fear has been my protection. There's no way to make anyone understand this. People or dogs – what's the difference when vibes are concerned? I send out good vibes – that's what comes back. Well, while I'm practically sitting in the street watching people walk by, Raphael drives by alone on his way to the victory celebration at the Hotel Bonaire. That solved my problem and relieved Rigoberto of responsibility. It was close to 1:00 a.m. when I got home, not tired anymore – excited, exhilarated – in spite of which I fell asleep at once and awoke, as usual, at 6:00 a.m.

Earlier yesterday Mrs Reed, the boys and I spent four delightful hours at the beach. I am almost brown enough to qualify as the mother of the two little brown boys; not yet able to claim the little Jamaican boys, though. I love it at the beach but I get green with envy as I see the beautiful young things in their bikinis. I would go to the beach every day but I'm chintzy about the taxi money so I'm going to settle for every other day – big sacrifice, yes? Of course not! This typing has become almost a compulsion. I see myself come alive and understandable as the words flow from the ribbon. I know it isn't creative or good writing but it gets out of me what would, for lack of anyone to share my thoughts with, stifle and choke me and leave me unfulfilled. If I spent more days at the beach, this would suffer and so would I, so it is no sacrifice to miss days at the beach. It is good and helps me to bring my life into balance.

This morning I am waiting for Rigoberto to show up – although when is a good guess. I suspect that, freed from the responsibility of getting me home, he joined the happy crowd and probably didn't get to bed until dawn. On second thoughts, he's much too mature – even at twenty-two – for kid stuff. He is strongly opposed to the way the Miss Teen contests are run. He feels that it is not youth but sex which is being offered or at least exploited. He sees no reason for the bikini showing and deplores the lack of preparation the girls get in handling the adulation they receive. He told of one 'Miss World' who is now in Belgium making porno films and feels that the girls are too young to be aware of the life they are setting out on. He was as shocked as I when a musical group known as African Blood did a number in English that I think would not have been allowed in the States. I doubt if many understood what was being said but knowing how the island kids love American rock – hard and soft – it is just possible that they do know. I couldn't believe what I was hearing and I'll spare you the words. There was, however, a marvelous entertainer, George Williams, who is the Tom Jones of the islands. He is great and I wanted to squeal with delight like the kids. He did three numbers and they would have kept him there all night – I would have too. He was dark and very handsome in that earthy, physical way smart entertainers develop. He, too, sold himself but he was a mature man who knew the score and was professional enough to know where to stop short of obscenity. A good show.

I am listening to the Brandenburgs again and I made a wonderful discovery. Jacqueline, the little eleven-year-old girl who spends a lot of time with me, is lying on my floor. She is practically under my feet as I type and she is enchanted with Bach. There are parts in the concerto that are almost dance tunes and while they were playing she got up and started to dance, first self-consciously, then with great abandon. Right now, during a quiet melodic part, she is quietly humming. Who says you have to cultivate a taste for Bach? Expose kids to it while they are pure and you've sold them. Anyway, it's like having a kitten under the table with her soft humming and the love I feel from her.

I found out from Mrs Reed that poor Mr Sweebie has been sick since last Tuesday. When I learned this I involuntarily exploded with, 'Oh, I'm glad he's sick!' Both Mr and Mrs Reed looked at me and when I realized how it must have sounded, I turned scarlet. In a minute, though, we were all laughing because we all knew that I really meant 'Oh, I'm glad he didn't just forget!'

August 5
8:00 *a.m.*

My friend Carlos Mercera has been moved from the hospital to an adjacent building which is the equivalent of an old-folks home. It is for the care of those old ones who still need some nursing care which they can't or won't get at home. It, too, is part of the Catholic convent but just how I haven't discovered. When I ask if it is part of the convent or church I am told, 'Well, not really.' When I ask if it is government supported I'm told, 'Well, not really.' What I do know is that Carlos is receiving tender and loving care. The director of the home came over to meet me and, as I left, she walked to the street with me and said, 'I hope you will come often to see him.' When I told her that I had been coming almost every day she was so pleased. I know that Carlos is most loved but I think the same kind of concern is given to others too.

I found Carlos sitting in a rocking-chair, dressed in

street clothes. His right side from shoulder to toes is paralyzed. Fortunately, his face was spared so he doesn't have that disfigurement. I got to the hospital at about 10:00 a.m. and he had already had a lot of company. There were two men and an old lady with him when I arrived. I made him laugh and got him to talk a little. Usually he just says, 'Yea, yea,' and no further response but I can make him laugh and talk a little. I am shameless in my display of affection for the old boy and he loves it. I saw that after awhile he was getting too tired. His head would droop and his eyes would close. I asked a nurse if he couldn't be put to bed and she went scurrying around, finally returning with the head nurse who explained to me that the doctor had ordered that he sit up until after lunch. Then he could be put to bed for only three hours, after which he was to be put in the chair again. I realized that the doctor was afraid of pneumonia if Carlos lay too long. Try to understand that all this conversation is going on in Papiamentu and that, while I lag behind in what is being said, I manage to catch up and understand.

I think my learning of Papiamentu will soon speed up. A very nice thing has happened. Betti, a daughter of Loie Martis who teaches school here on Bonaire and has been to Holland on vacation, wants me to teach her English. She did learn English in high school – four years of it – and speaks very well but she is dissatisfied (just as Raphael is) because it is so stiff and bookish. They had no conversational English at all. I agreed, on the condition that we spend a part of every lesson on Papiamentu. We had our first lesson yesterday and I am using the dialogue method. I have typed out a series of ordinary, easy conversations that might take place between any two people – on a variety of subjects. The language is natural and familiar. For instance, she said that they were taught that upon being introduced one said, 'How do you do?' or 'Enchanted'. Now I ask you, what two Americans being introduced would say such things? She had no understanding of the word 'nice'. It took a little exploring to find the Papiamentu equivalent – 'casi bon', which literally means 'almost good'. It's going to be fun, besides which I did get a chance to tell her a little about the Faith and shall probably be able to do more.

Raphael is very angry with me and I am highly amused. The day after the Miss Teen contest he asked me how his English had been. I told him that it was excellent but made the mistake of saying that there had been one word he had mispronounced. When he asked which word it was I had to tell him that I couldn't remember, that it was so unimportant, that even TV announcers often made mistakes, that it just didn't occur to me to make a special note of it. He was furious.

'If I make a mistake, it's your fault! You should have teached me better!'

At that, I just fell apart. He is so proud and such a perfectionist but it WAS so funny. If he hadn't been so angry, he would never have made THAT grammatical error!

Sunday, while Rigoberto was here, we tried to phone everyone on the list Mr Mázgání had given me. We weren't able to reach anyone. The plan was that, since Rigo can speak whatever language is needed, he would at least be able to explain just where I live and set up some firm commitments.

It seems that every attempt I make to contact people is

abortive. I'm sure I don't know why. I have no choice but to keep trying and accept whatever comes of my efforts. I haven't followed through with my plan to hire a taxi every other day because I don't know where to have the driver take me. It's all very frustrating and makes me dissatisfied with myself. I don't want to set the island on fire, I just want to light a teeny little candle. I keep asking myself, 'Is it enough that I am loved if I can't turn that love to Bahá'u'lláh? How much longer can I continue to get so much more than I give?' These are disquieting thoughts and are guaranteed to lower my effectiveness, so I try very hard to shake them. I wish I really understood just what pioneering is. If, as Horace Holley is alleged to have said, it is the moving from an old self to a new self, I have probably made it, but I cannot accept that the answer is that easy. There must be some very concrete and real reasons for keeping a lone Bahá'í in a place where no results are shown for so long. I know very well the story of Africa where the seeds were planted but lay dormant for so many years, finally to emerge and blossom. Isn't it rather late for that now, in 1975, just 25 years short of the end of the century? I don't question the wisdom of my being here; I just wish I understood it more fully. I have written to the International Goals Committee that teaching the Faith here is no different from anywhere in the States:

> My feeling is that the best way to make progress here would be to find a Dutch couple who would get a teaching job here, either he or she. It would be very good if they had children of school age. Dutch is the official language and all school-children speak it. With Dutch, everyone reachable could be reached. A family

would so readily be accepted by Bonairians to whom families are still very important. There are many Dutch school-teachers here. I don't know how they go about getting teaching jobs but I know they do get three-year contracts. One such family could do more for the Faith than a dozen Rhodas or Marions.

If I had my large Bahá'í library and were able to do the necessary research, I would spend the time preparing course material. I still feel that my greatest value to the Faith lies in my speaking and teaching abilities which stagnate here. I know there will be those who say that just to live the life is to teach – but is it, when there are other things one can do also? I'm sure I'll have time to resolve these questions before I leave the island and that, when the time comes to leave, I shall be very unhappy. I hope that whatever the reason for God guiding me to serve here, it will become manifest when I return. It is just occurring to me that perhaps I'm being put on ice, as it were, because of the heat of the fire with which I burn to teach. It is just possible that my need to teach is an ego thing which needs cooling. I can accept that because I am only too aware of the glow and satisfaction I get from the adulation and praise my public efforts receive. Could be my material self got too big for my spiritual breeches and one or the other has to be altered!

Same day
5:30 p.m.

I SPENT three and a half hours at the beach alone because Mrs Reed – black as she is – suffered a rather bad sunburn from our previous day at the beach. I am browning beautifully and loving it but she, poor love, is in misery. I took my tape recorder and read and listened to Bach, Beethoven and Schubert and allowed myself to be made love to by an adoring sun. I didn't even go near the water today. Just baking in the sun and having my senses of sight, sound and mind enriched was enough. Water I can get from the shower at home.

Betti Martis just left. We had a pretty good lesson. After we had read and fully discussed the three dialogues I had written in English we did them in Papiamentu. It was much easier than I had imagined it would be and we got along fine.

August 6
7:30 p.m.

It's blowing pretty hard outside which makes sitting on the veranda not too pleasant. It looks as if another storm may be in the making, so I'll try some night writing.

Today I was finally discharged by the doctor. I have healed beautifully with not too much of a scar. Maybe I'll try for 'Mrs World' after all! Dr Welvaart is a gentleman. I must have made at least ten visits to his office, most of them requiring some special attention from him, which I would rather have done without. Each time a salve or ointment was applied – and bandages. I was really beginning to worry about paying him, the more so when I found a bill from the hospital for 20 guilders for the two dressings they did. 20 guilders is about US$11.00, so I really dreaded the doctor's bill. He only charged me 35 guilders and, when I showed him the bill from the hospital, he said it was too much and to tell them he said so – and to show them his bill. I sat in his office for three hours today, the longest time yet and as I looked around at the people waiting so patiently and listened to the talk – all in Papiamentu – I realized that I was beginning to understand little snatches of conversation from this group and that. I remembered that there had been many times when I'd had opportunities to mention the Faith while sitting out those long waits. I saw the honey I could distill out of THAT bitter poison and I was almost glad of the suffering! I saw that I had been given a chance to be with people I would not ordinarily have met and that I was privileged to be a part of the island life that many visitors miss. So chalk up another experience for Mme Pioneer – chalk up another adventure and more enrichment.

It's strange that the night writing isn't coming too easily. Nights seem to be the time for reflection and not action. I kind of sort out my thoughts at night and let 'em rip early in the morning.

August 9
7:10 p.m.

It is night again and I'm going to give it another try. I have just taken two flash pictures of the evening sky and used the last two flash cubes I had. Now I'm kicking myself because in just exactly thirty seconds, the colors have become unbelievable. What I thought was so great thirty seconds ago has paled against the brilliance of the now! Even as I type these words, the color is fading and the sky is quickly darkening. I'm typing because it has started to rain heavily and I am unable to sit outside.

I have had a very exciting and wonderful day! Last

week I received a letter from the Regional Teaching Committee of the Islands advising me that possibly on Saturday (today) a small plane would be arriving at the Flamingo Airport bringing a Mr Vernhout, a traveling teacher and member of the National Teaching Committee of Holland. The non-Bahá'í husband of the secretary of the RTC was flying his own little sport plane in, bringing Mr Vernhout to the island. I was to call Curaçao on Friday to confirm this. When I called, there was just a message for me saying that they would arrive at 9:45 a.m. I had no idea how long they would stay or what plans Mr Vernhout had, so I could do nothing more than be at the airport to meet them. Mr Lenderink, the pilot, had one of his younger daughters and a friend of hers with him. It was their plan to go to one of the beaches. Mr Vernhout was simply going to spend the day with me.

I hope the pictures I took of Mr Vernhout are good because he is so handsome, so charming and so utterly in love with the Faith that he actually glows with love and radiance. He teaches at a college in Holland but somehow it didn't seem important to ask what he taught. Beloved Auxiliary Board member Mr Mázgání had urged him to travel teach in the Netherlands Antilles during his vacation and he had been on St Maarten, Saba, Aruba and Curaçao. He told me such marvelous stories of the successes in these places that I cried with joy. He had been 28 days on Aruba. When he arrived, there were two resident Bahá'ís. By the time he left there had been twenty-eight enrollments. He is so modest, he insists that he had only a small part to play in the successes. He told of almost miraculous things that brought first one, then another and another to hear him.

He credits most of the success to the first woman to declare. He says she brought the others. His modesty is no sham, no phony piety. It is real and he is so real.

What a shot in the arm this has been for me. I can now understand so much better why when I went travel-teaching I was greeted with hugs and kisses and left with tears. I apologized for not making any plans and he quickly assured me that his entire reason for coming was just to share Bahá'í love and fellowship with me. And that he did. We had some prayers together – and, oh, how much better they sounded. We played the beautiful tape of the Sparks Feast. He told me how he became a Bahá'í and it sounded like some impossible dream. He told me of his travels and brought me the love of the friends in Curaçao. I fixed lunch for us, then at 3:00 p.m. Mr Lenderink arrived in a rented car, as pre-arranged, to pick him up and go back to the airport. Mr Vernhout is going to try to come back during his Christmas vacation, though I'm beginning to wonder if that would be a good time. If it works out, then we'll assume it is. If he comes, I will have had time to work out some meetings for him whether I shall be here then or not. I think the most wonderful thing he did for me was to tell me that the successes on Aruba and other places were not won during his visit but were the result of years of pioneering efforts. He begged me not to denigrate my efforts or my service and to read the passage from the front of the prayer book which I quote here:

> Intone, O My servant, the verses of God that have been received by thee, as intoned by them who have drawn nigh unto Him, that the sweetness of thy melody may kindle thine own soul, and attract the hearts of all men.

> Whoso reciteth, in the privacy of his chamber, the verses revealed by God, the scattering angels of the Almighty shall scatter abroad the fragrance of the words uttered by his mouth, and shall cause the heart of every righteous man to throb. Though he may, at first, remain unaware of its effect, yet the virtue of the grace vouchsafed unto him must needs sooner or later exercise its influence upon his soul. Thus have the mysteries of the Revelation of God been decreed by virtue of the will of Him Who is the Source of power and wisdom.
>
> *Bahá'u'lláh*

I think we do tend to forget, and we need to be reminded, that our prayers have great and powerful effect and that praying, if nothing else is possible, is a great and meritorious service. I feel so much better. Oh, to be sure I had told myself all that – but it sounded so good from another!

August 10
8:30 a.m.

Of all the days of the week this is the one I dread the most because it is the one day when my solitude becomes oppressive. It has been bad on other Sundays but today is worse because of the contrast with yesterday. Yesterday, with the loving companionship of Gerrit Vernhout, I enjoyed an exchange of thought and feeling. Today, with the knowledge that there will be no one to share with, the day seems endless and fruitless. I am learning at first hand what I have mouthed for so many years: that without the support of community life we are bound to wither and weaken. It may horrify you to hear the thought that has just come into my mind: that in a way we commit spiritual cannibalism with each other – that is, we feed on one another spiritually. We seem to have a spiritual hunger that can best be sustained by drawing on the spiritual reserves of another. To be a lone, isolated Bahá'í is to suffer spiritual malnutrition. There is no doubt that the prayers and readings support and strengthen us but it is like the vitamins and food supplements we take – it is necessary that solid, real food be also taken. To a believer in an isolated spot, the letters of the friends are highly supportive. Without them – and without actual contact with other believers – the isolated Bahá'í falls victim to his own imaginings and can very easily decline from strength to weakness. Once the power of the community is really understood, no one would ever separate himself from it; every lone Bahá'í would give up rest and sleep in order to surround himself quickly with a community; every community would purify and strengthen itself in order to provide the maximum security and peace for the believers. Oh, how I long to be back once more in a community – any community, no matter how weak, how immature, how undeveloped administratively. Even the rubbing together of the cockle-burrs would be a joy because I know that only after the friction does the smoothness come – and I would even welcome the friction.

I'd better get on another tack or I'll end up in sad and longing tears instead of tears of gratitude for being permitted to see these things so clearly. It is as if I were being told, 'All right, you've taught these things for years from your head; now know them from your heart.'

Tropical heat has finally descended upon the island

and, for the first time in my life, I am experiencing sweat – not polite perspiration but SWEAT. My dear friend Jane Ward used to be annoyed with me because when everyone else was dripping wet with the heat I remained cool and dry. She was sure it was highly unusual for me not to perspire a little. Well, this stuff running down my face is not ice water! Without the gentle trade winds, I think people would go a little mad with such heat. It helps to understand the temperament and the customs of tropical people – to experience the heat and what it does. It helps one understand the difference between northern and southern cultures. I'm beginning to learn to walk a little slower because people think it's silly to stride out with arms swinging as if on dress parade. I'm learning to move a little slower and to respond a little slower. A very welcome result has been the lowering of my blood pressure to absolutely normal.

I have been assuring Tom that he would love it here and that he would live ten years longer; now I'm trying to analyze that to see if it is true. One would not be happy here unless one were willing to experience an entirely new way of life. Part of the quality of the peace that surrounds us here is that we live in a world apart from the bigger world. Our problems are local problems and they are solved locally. We are aware of the rest of the world: we do get newspapers and magazines, we do have limited TV and lots of radio but we are not committed to them. In fact, I think we don't even care too much. I think if all communication with the rest of the world were cut off we on Bonaire would go on living in the same way, taking care of ourselves and our families.

This does not mean that we are isolationists. There

just doesn't seem to be the emotional and enervating involvement in world affairs. Since the papers and TV programs are largely in Spanish and the English papers arrive weeks after they are printed, Tom might be unhappy at not having his finger on the pulse of the world. I don't know, of course, that this is true. He might take to Bonaire like a seagull to the air. I do think it is important, though, for anyone contemplating pioneering to honestly evaluate his need of the world: to ask himself whether he needs the stimulation of television, the theatre, libraries; whether he is dependent on the company of family and friends and how much solitude he can bear.

I am anxiously looking forward to my visit to Curaçao next week. I have already bought my plane ticket. I go on Sunday night and shall, hopefully, come back on the ferry Thursday night. Although I had planned to go on Monday and return on Wednesday, I had to change those plans when I discovered that the ferry doesn't come back on Wednesday but on Thursday and the only plane out on Monday is that little job I flew in on. I am awaiting a reply from Dr Rabbani about the possibility of staying the four nights with her. I will be there for the Feast of Asmá'.

August 12
8:30 a.m.

BUREAUCRACY is bureaucracy the world over, I guess. This morning there are seven men outside my house. They arrived in a truck at 8:00. Two of them seem to be doing something. One is drilling with one of those noisy, high-powered electric drills; the other is shoveling the loosened stuff. The other five are sitting around watching. Now, that's just about the way in the States too. Five sidewalk-superintend while one or two do the work. Oh, it's OK because they work for the government and isn't the government supposed to create jobs for the people? I haven't any idea what they are doing out at the side of the house. Their work isn't on the land on which my house is built so I'm sure it hasn't anything to do with me. I was just amused to see that nationality, language, customs – nothing seems to interfere with or change the way bureaucracy operates. It was the same when a small patch of the dirt road on which I live needed some pot-holes filled in. A heavy storm had washed a couple of big holes in the road and the highway department sent a crew of eight men to work on it. First, they had to wait until a truck brought dirt and stones to fill the holes. They waited about three hours for the first load. They were not the least bit unhappy. They had a radio and a jug and sat in the shade of some divi-divi trees and rested. When the dirt was dropped on the road, two of the men took turns shoveling it in place. The rest continued to earn salary by sitting it out. Then they all had to wait for the second load to be brought. This went on all day until finally the small patch was filled in and the men left with the comfortable knowledge that they had done a day's work. Is it any different at home?

Yesterday when I went to see Carlos in the 'Home', I was alone with him and had a chance to really talk with him. While we were talking and, as usual, I was making him laugh, the doctor came by and stood behind Carlos. He motioned to me to keep on talking and not to let Carlos know he was there. Carlos was unhappy. He said that there was nothing they could do for him and I tried to show him that now was the time for his faith to make itself evident. He is a faithful church-goer; a very devout and good man. I put it to him that all the years of piety were wasted if, now when the test came, he couldn't draw on his faith. He seemed to accept this and, at this point, the doctor made his presence known.

This is a different doctor. He is island born. I introduced myself to him and told him what a good friend Carlos is to me. I said I wished I could do something for him. The doctor replied that what I was doing was the very best thing that could be done. He said it was more valuable than the physical therapy.

He turned to Carlos and said, 'Mrs West is your very good friend and tells me that you have been very kind to her. Why don't you be kind to her now and show her that you CAN move your hand?'

Carlos looked from one to the other of us and wanly smiled.

The doctor said, 'Come on, Carlos, shake hands with her.' Both the doctor and I were so happy to see that Carlos did really try and that he was able to move the fingers of his poor paralyzed hand. The doctor was so pleased and, of course, tears filled my eyes.

I said to Carlos, 'Tell the doctor what my name is and where I come from.'

'This is Mrs West. She comes from Oklahoma,' Carlos answered.

I laughed and said, 'Carlos, I hope you moved my husband too. Oklahoma is close but not close enough. Can you do better?'

He chuckled and said, 'I guess I mean Nevada.'

When I was leaving, the doctor came to me and

explained that they had been worried because they thought he had suffered brain damage and this was the first indication that he was able to remember and to think clearly. I think it is because of the years of separation from his family that they haven't been able to reach him. Anyway, it was a good morning. The doctor seemed to feel that, with encouragement and cooperation from Carlos, in a month he might regain at least partial use of his limbs. I pray so! Carlos may never accept Bahá'u'lláh in this world but I cannot believe that Bahá'u'lláh isn't pouring down His love on this dear old man who has, since leaving the sea and the ways of the sea, given his life to the service of his fellow man.

August 13
3:30 p.m.

YESTERDAY I had suggested to the doctor that perhaps it would be helpful to Carlos if he had a little rubber ball to squeeze in the right hand. The doctor said, 'That would be the best thing.' I said that I would try to find one and bring it when I came the next day.

Well, I spent all morning asking in every shop on the island for a rubber ball. There just wasn't one to be had. I found soccer balls and ping-pong balls and beach balls but no small rubber or sponge ball. I finally settled for some large foam-rubber hair rollers as a temporary thing until I go to Curaçao – where I'm sure I can get what he needs. I put one of the rollers in his right hand and it worked fairly well but he didn't have enough to fight against. One of the nurses is going to tie two of them together to see if that works better.

Often when I visit Carlos, I find a man there whose

name, I have learned, is Umberto. He lives very near where I live and occasionally he has given me lifts to or from town. He was at the Home today and we both left at the same time. He offered to drive me home but I had some errands to do first and he kindly suggested that he had time and wouldn't mind running me around. I learned that he teaches at the Technical School here and, since school is on a short vacation until August 18th, he is free. When I heard 'Technische Scul' I remembered that Mr Mázgání had given me the name of a teacher at that school and I had tried unsuccessfully to find someone who knew him.

I asked Umberto about him.

'Of course, he is my friend and teaches at the school.'

I told Umberto that I was a Bahá'í and why I was on the island, that Mr Scherpton's name had been given to me to contact. Umberto said that he would see him tomorrow because there was a staff meeting prior to school opening and that he would give him the message.

'I have heard about the Bahá'í Faith but I never found anybody who could tell me about it.'

I gave him a pamphlet in Papiamentu and told him I was there for just that purpose – to tell about the Bahá'í Faith – and that I hoped he would give me the opportunity to do that. Now – how about that? This morning when I awoke, I told myself that maybe I hadn't prayed hard enough, or long enough, or humbly enough and this morning my prayers would blister the walls with their power. I guess I HADN'T prayed hard enough, long enough or humbly enough because – when I really pushed MYSELF away and nothing but the soul was there to cry out – look what happened!

August 17
3:30 p.m.

I AM waiting for Umberto to take me to the airport where I shall make the short flight (15 minutes) to Curaçao. I am very anxious to get there because something is starting to happen to the other side of my back that feels just like the way the cyst began. I want Dr Rabbani to look at it and, hopefully, do something before it gets too bad. I hope I don't have to go through that again.

August 22

I WANT to tell you about my visit to Curaçao but I'm going to start at the end because it gave me a chance to learn something more about the way of life here. As I understand it, it is the way of life generally found in the countries south of our US border.

I had planned to return by boat but was warned that the boat schedule was erratic. How erratic I could not possibly have guessed – and thereby hangs this tale. On Wednesday, the day before my planned return, I called to ask about the departure time. I was informed that the boat left at 1:00 p.m. I asked how long the trip took and was told three hours and that arrival at Bonaire was 4:00 p.m. On hearing this I asked if there was a later boat and was told that there was only the one. Then I said that there must be some mistake because, in Bonaire, I was told the ferry didn't arrive until 9:00 or 10:00 p.m.

'That's right,' replied the clerk.

'Now wait a minute,' said I, 'that doesn't figure. If the boat leaves at 1:00 p.m. and takes three hours to get there, how could it possibly arrive at 9:00 or 10:00 p.m.?'

'Well,' replies the gal, 'it doesn't always leave at 1:00 p.m.'

I asked, 'How will I know when to come to the pier then?'

'Well, you had better call here at 12:00 noon and we will know,' was her answer.

On Thursday, Dr Rabbani, my hostess, was preparing lunch for us and I asked Rigoberto to call the dock and find out the departure time. He did and was told that we had to be there at once. Lunch was put aside and we got into the car and flew to the pier. When we got there I didn't see any boat and rushed to the ticket window and asked if I had missed it.

'Oh no, the boat won't leave until 6:00 p.m.'

I BLEW MY STACK!

'Why were we told to get down here at noon? Surely you knew ten minutes ago that the boat wasn't in and wouldn't leave until 6:00?'

'Yes,' she said, 'but you have to buy your ticket now.'

I looked around and saw three women, surrounded by shopping bags and suitcases, patiently sitting on piles of lumber – just sitting. There was nothing but a covered pier – no seats, no benches, no snack bar – nothing, but nothing. The stack was still blowing and I asked what we were expected to do until 6:00. I was told that I could go home or go to Punda (that's what the shopping area is called on Curaçao).

I said, 'Thank you very much. I'll take the plane.' I was shaking with anger and it wasn't until I got back in the car that I realized my anger was ill-directed at that poor clerk; so I went back in and apologized as well as I could – because I still hadn't really cooled off. We drove back to Nosrat's (Dr Rabbani), finished fixing lunch and settled down to wait for the plane. I could have gone on the little plane at 4:00 but, sissy that I am, I decided on the 8:00 plane because it is a nice, big, substantial-looking job. I arrived home at 8:30, having asked the taxi to stop first at the post office for my mail.

My stay in Curaçao was delightful, spoiled only by the development of another 'whatever it was', this time under the right shoulder-blade. Fortunately, we got it at the very start and I had the constant attention of my wonderful doctor hostess. She applied very hot compresses (sterile, of course) and salve dressings until the darn thing came to a head and opened. After that began the same torturous scraping and digging as before except that Nosrat was so gentle and took a long time to avoid as much pain as possible. Because we caught it early the infection was not deep and didn't give me any fever or really very much pain – except at digging time. I cannot imagine what is causing these things. I have never in my life had so much as a pimple – and now, in rapid succession, two 'things'. If I were home I would have some blood testing done. That will have to wait and I can only pray that 'number two' is the last. This one is not healed and I must have daily dressings which my friend Mrs Martis will do.

Now, finally, Curaçao! I arrived Sunday evening and spent a wonderful time with Nosrat – just talking. She lives alone too. Because all of the other Bahá'ís have families it makes her the 'odd-man-out' in the community. She is afire with the love of the Faith. When the other Bahá'ís are busy and unable to attend a meeting, Nosrat is alone.

She was as pleased to have me to talk to as I was to listen. She told me fascinating stories of her life in Persia and of her pioneering adventures. Now SHE'S a real pioneer! At 18 she volunteered to go as a teacher to a remote village in Iran where Bahá'ís were hated. Her experiences there for a year would make a great book. Just as the few Bahá'ís there were being severely persecuted, an army colonel who just happened to be a Bahá'í was transferred to that area and was able to get all the Bahá'ís out safely. That was just one of the minor miracles that happened in that year. From that time on, except for taking the time to study and become a doctor, her life has been spent in one remote and foreign place after another. She is terrific. I listened to her that Sunday night until 2:00 a.m.

On Monday Rigoberto came for me and we walked to Punda and shopped. The shopping is absolutely fantastic. One shop after another – block after block – loaded with all the goods of the world. Prices are very reasonable because everything is duty free. In every shop I saw things that I wanted for each of you. I would spot something and say to myself, 'That would be great for – –.' But of course I didn't dare be tempted. I did buy a big box of marvelous chocolates for the Martis family. (Loie has been feeding my cats and turning the night light on and off.) I also bought a dress and some cheap jewelry for my little friend Jacqueline. I found just the right size ball for Carlos and, aside from a few inexpensive drug items, that was the extent of my shopping. But it took three fun-filled days to do it! Rigo is a delightful shopping companion and we had lots of fun together. One day I sat in on his Papiamentu class. He is a language teacher.

Tuesday night was a Feast and there were two new believers welcomed that night. One is a beautiful young man of twenty-four and the other a woman of about thirty-five. Both are native believers – which is so great. Curaçao now has at least four native believers. There are one or two others but they are not as active. The Feast was another international experience. Prayers were said in English, Papiamentu, Spanish, Dutch and Persian. Consultation was lively and spirited. It was a good Feast and I had needed it badly. There were twelve of us. Refreshments were very simple. The Feast was in Nosrat's house and she doesn't believe in having the social hour overshadow the devotional hour.

The next night, Wednesday, was the Regional Teaching Committee meeting. It was held in the beautiful home of a Dutch couple who are leaving this month to return to Holland. The husband, Wouter Bos, is an internist in psychiatry. He had served his year in a hospital here and must return to Holland for accreditation (I think that's right). Actually, they have been on Curaçao for two years – for the sake of the Faith – but only one year counts for his medical credit. It was a very exciting meeting because sparks flew and opinions clashed. It was just like home. However there is evidently a great deal of love and unity – as indeed there would have to be to keep these five absolutely different personality types working together for so long. It was decided to send me on a week-end teaching trip to Aruba, where the Faith has just come alive due to the visit of Gerrit Vernhout.

He had twenty-eight declarations and there are enough for two assemblies. I am going to do a pre-assembly deepening. The date has not been decided. Aruba will be asked to select a date. Also they asked me to serve on the committee – with the permission of the National Spiritual Assembly of Venezuela. I suggested that I would rather be used as a resource person and not be on the committee officially. It seems so silly for just four months.

On Wednesday Nosrat didn't work because she had developed an ear infection which was not only very painful but prevented her from using her stethoscope. Much of her work is in preventive medicine with the small school children. She tells me that every child of school age gets free medical service and that it is mandatory that parents follow up on any treatment or medication the child is given. She says she doesn't know anyplace else in the world where such a program is being practiced. She also tells me that they have practically wiped out most of the children's diseases. It is because of this program that she stays here and puts up with the awful bureaucratic shenanigans of any such program. She is, essentially, a 'loner' and would just like to get the work done without the rigamarole found in any government office the world over.

Thursday morning and then later in the afternoon, while we waited for me to go to the airport, we just talked. She told me about her trip up the Amazon with Amatu'l-Bahá Rúḥíyyih Khánum. For instance, for twenty-eight days they slept in hammocks – the two women and eight men. Rúḥíyyih Khánum did a lot of the cooking. The privy was a tiny enclosed section at the end of the boat, hanging over the water. She had pictures of all this. It was very primitive and I know that I could never have made that trip. Rúḥíyyih Khánum said she did it to show that if she could do it at her age, then 65 years old, others could do it. But not everyone was such a tomboy as she was as a child! She was evidently being prepared to be what she is now. She sets a mighty pace for the rest of us.

Now I want to tell you a little about Curaçao itself. If you were to drive all around it, I don't think you would rack up 100 miles. It is larger than Bonaire but still a small island. Those fabulous shops are located in an area known as the Punda. Across the St Anna Bay lies the Otrabanda (literally, the other side). The two sides are connected by a unique bridge – a pontoon bridge. The original bridge was the suggestion of an American consul and, with his help, was built in 1888. He also brought electricity and a water purifying plant to the island. Like Bonaire, it is a desert island but it has a much more varied landscape than Bonaire. It is interesting to note that Peter Stuyvesant, at the age of 26, was the first Director of the ABC Islands. He later became the Director of New Amsterdam, which was to become New York City.

Curaçao is much different from Bonaire. It is a very busy, bustling place, heavily populated. There are more than 140,000 people here representing some 79 nationalities. The largest group are the native Curaçaoans, about 106,000. It has a very large Jewish population, Jews having fled from Portugal and Spain during the oppressions there. These are Sephardic Jews; that is, not East European. The Jews have been very effective in raising the standard of living in the islands. There is also a Muslim community with its own mosque. Traffic in

Willemstad, the chief city, is unbelievable. It is almost like peak hours in Chicago and the drivers must have taken lessons from the Persians. It's every man for himself. The gentlest person becomes a maniac behind the wheel of a car. There doesn't seem to be any right of way – the whole idea of driving here is to get there first and bluff your way through. It's a hair-raising experience to be a passenger. Add to this the fact that Nosrat IS Persian and you can imagine the wild rides I had with her.

Curaçao would be unbelievable on a picture postcard. Houses are painted every color imaginable and some that cannot be imagined. There is a legend about those varied-colored houses. It is said that one of the early governors was plagued by headaches. He became convinced that the glare from the then whitewashed houses was responsible and ordered that all buildings had to be immediately painted some color. From afar, they look like toy houses frosted with that awful commercial, colored frosting that says, 'The cake can't possibly taste as bad as it looks – so go on, take a bite.'

The natives on Curaçao are also beautiful, like the Bonairians. The men are so tall and straight and handsome; the girls are very pretty and there are not too many obese people. Pride of island is very strong. To the Curaçaoans, there is no island like Curaçao and there is much rivalry between the islanders. This was very strongly evident at the Miss Teen contest. Each contestant had her own clack – that is, cheering section. It was like a national political convention.

I have discovered that Papiamentu is rooted in Portuguese and the Portuguese verb 'papear' means 'to jabber' or 'to chatter', and it is believed by some experts that there's where Papiamentu got its name. One language scholar calls it 'pidgin everything'. There is, as yet, no fixed spelling and even among the three islands there are many strong differences in the way the words are used and sentences are structured.

I am now most anxious to see Aruba.

August 28

I WANT to tell you about a little girl named Jacqueline. I'm not sure I can tell it right. I'm not very good yet at this kind of writing, but Jacqueline has taken hold of me in such a way that I feel almost as though she lives in me and maybe I can do her justice.

Jacqueline is one of fourteen children in the 'Papa Diek' family. She certainly is not the prettiest, nor is she the most docile and well-behaved. She is considered to be a 'problem' to her family and it has even been said that she is 'crazy'. She is not one of the children that I 'fell in love with' and I had not singled her out for any special attention. She had singled me out, though, and from the start she made it plain that she was cultivating me.

The children in that family came from I don't know how many fathers but from one mother. They have a strong sense of family and are fiercely protective of one another. Jacqueline, who is twelve, has either appointed herself, or has been appointed, protector and guardian for the younger children who range in age from one year old to eleven, and there are nine in number. The mother produced fifteen children in twenty years and is still going strong. The youngest is just one year old and Mrs Franz still has a lot of zing left. It seems, however, that though she can produce the children she doesn't know how to mother them – and this care they give each other.

For reasons that I haven't yet sorted out, Jacqueline has a kind of scapegoat position in the family and she is the one at whom most of the screaming and cursing is done by the mother. It is Jacqueline who 'runs away' every day for at least half an hour and I sometimes see her sobbing in the bushes behind my house. However, it wasn't until she had crept into my heart that I began to notice that. Let me see if I can recall how our friendship started.

I told you that the children would descend on me *en masse* and they would jabber away at me until my head would spin. I couldn't understand a word of what they were saying and none of them seemed to understand why they weren't getting appropriate responses; no one, that is, except Jacqueline. She would get the children quiet and very very patiently, try to make me understand. Sometimes she would take my hand and lead me to an object to show me what they were saying. Patiently she would repeat, slowly and carefully, a word I had failed to get. Without putting me down at all and without any sense of superiority, she would say, 'Bo ta comprende?' (Do you understand?) She led me as carefully and gently as one would lead a child. I found that

I was looking forward to these unplanned learning sessions.

The other children soon tired of the 'stupid' American lady. Oh, not that they ever said that – and perhaps they didn't even think that – but it was apparent that it wasn't fun any longer. It stopped being productive for them when I stopped buying huge bags of candy to divide among them. I caught on to this little ploy almost at once but went along with it because they were so darned cute and I did want them around – for awhile, at least. (See how we exploit one another – even when it is as innocent as this!)

Jacqueline never dropped away. She came every day. Sometimes she came while I was cleaning house or washing dishes. She always helped without asking if she might. She just pitched in and helped. I began to notice a Cinderella quality about her – a wistful looking at things and wanting. Her clothes were ragged and obviously hand-me-downs. She wasn't always too clean; she always seemed hungry. Her brother Karel, the one I have previously referred to as a little Greek temple boy, had been coming quite often too when I decided to use them to work for me and to pay them. I made the offer that if Karel watered my yard every day and Jacqueline kept my windows clean, I would pay them one guilder each week. They danced and squealed with delight and have been faithful in their duties ever since.

But this isn't really telling about Jacqueline!

From the beginning, it was clear that she was watching everything I did with an eye to doing just as I did. I had only to show her once what I meant by a clean window and she'd practically wear the glass out polishing and cleaning. She loved to wash my dishes but I wouldn't allow that until I was sure she REALLY washed them.

I had a few bad moments with her because she was so unabashed that she would, very casually, ask me to give her things or buy her things. I had to get Rigoberto, when he was here, to supplement my bad Papiamentu with some good hard talk about not asking for things. I told her that I would give her anything that I wanted to give her but I would not give her anything she asked for. She didn't get my message until Rigo laid it on her. After that if any of the kids even looked as if they were about to ask for 'mangel' or 'biscutis' (candy or cookies), she would shush them and say, 'Bo no ta pidi' – 'You don't ask'.

She became fiercely protective of me and my privacy. She had learned that I don't like an audience when I eat, so she would sit outside and keep the others away. She knew how thoroughly I deplored the screaming and yelling that went on around us and because I had said so often to her, 'Dem mi cas, papia cu stem abou' – 'In my house, speak with a soft voice', she would say this to the children if they were loud and noisy around the house. I wouldn't have shushed them but she did! She had also observed that I need to concentrate when I'm typing and she would sit on the floor near my feet very quietly and, if there was a threatened invasion by the others, she would quickly go to the outside gate and tell them that the Señora was working. She seemed to understand that this was work although I had never told her so. All this sensitivity from a little girl who was labeled 'slow', 'queer' and 'crazy'. This is the little girl who has learned to love Bach and Schubert and asks me to play them while she sits at my feet and hums or gets up and, softly and unselfconsciously, dances. This is the little girl who when her step-father, Papa Diek, was hurt in an accident the day before yesterday, asked me to take her to the hospital to see him.

This morning very early she came to the house. I had made it very clear to her yesterday, when she asked me if she could walk to the *playa* with me and if I would take her to see Papa Diek, that if she went with me she would have to wear shoes and clean herself properly. When she arrived this morning she was scrubbed and shining. She had washed her hair and had had someone braid it for her. She looked so sweet that I took a picture of her on the way to the *playa*.

We got to the hospital much too early so we visited with Carlos for awhile and then went to find Papa. He was not a very pretty sight. He had fallen from a high truck on his face – no, I don't think he was drunk – and had knocked out several teeth and bruised his nose and mouth. His lips were swollen and his eyes were blacked. He seemed to be in great pain and said he had been given no sedation of any kind. I saw Jacqueline's eyes widen with horror as she looked at him and she drew back from the bed. I stayed for only a moment longer and followed her outside where I found her, leaning against the wall, sobbing. I had to get one of the nurses, who speaks quite good English, to assure her that Papa was not as bad as he looked and that he would be all right – as I'm sure he will be. Jacqueline continued to cry until I asked the nurse to tell her that she was making me feel guilty at having brought her and that if she didn't try to stop crying I would probably cry too. At this she looked at me – long and deeply – drew a deep breath, wiped her eyes with the back of her hand and gave me the faintest, weakest smile I have ever seen – but she did stop crying.

I'll tell you something else about this little girl. School is once again in session and Jacqueline wanted some felt-tipped pens and a school bag very much. When she asked for them at home, there ensued one of the most violent and noisy scenes on record. Mrs Franz screamed invectives and curses for hours. Finally Jacqueline 'ran away' with Mrs Franz hurling bitter words after her. Of course, I dared not interfere but later that evening Jacqueline and her little half-sister Connie came to see me and to ask me to write a letter to Jacqueline's father who lives on St Maarten and speaks English. I was to tell him that Jacqueline wanted a school bag and some pens. I couldn't do that but I couldn't make them understand why. She insisted that, since I wrote English and her father understood English, there should be no problem. I hadn't enough Papiamentu to make her understand that I couldn't interfere in a family matter – that I didn't want to do anything to get the mother on my back – that I dreaded her anger and resentment. Finally I asked her to come to the Martis' with me and there I asked Betti to explain it to Jacqueline. While Betti was talking, Jacqueline watched me. As she began to understand, her belligerent, angry look softened and after a little while she took my hand and said, 'Bini' – 'Come', as if I were the one to be protected. And that has been our relationship.

It was strange. When I first tried to make her understand that she mustn't ask for things, I could see the wheels turning and I knew she was thinking, 'Well, if I don't ask for things, how is this simple-minded woman going to know what I want? If I don't say what

I like, how will she know?' If I had any candy or cookies in the house, she really couldn't see why she shouldn't ask for them. What were candy and cookies for if not to eat? It is this kind of direct simplicity that I find so honest and appealing. No tricks – no game playing – just simple, honest and direct. What a price we pay for our 'civilization'. My little girl named Jacqueline is teaching me more than Papiamentu!

I remember writing, many weeks ago when I first met the children, that I had fallen in love with one little girl with a couple of teeth missing and a little boy with black curly hair, that I wondered how I could isolate them from the rest without causing hurt feelings. Well, I didn't have to do anything. It just happened. Karel is the boy and Connie is the little girl. Jacqueline has a better relationship with Karel and Connie than with any of the others and doesn't mind sharing 'her Señora' with these two. Connie was very shy at first – strangely enough, Jacqueline and Karel were never shy with me. Gradually Connie warmed up and just a couple of days ago she was whispering to Jacqueline and giggling. When I asked why, she got all flustered but Jacqueline practically ordered her to tell me what she had said. Shyly, sweetly, Connie raised her eyes.

'Mi ta gusta Señora. Mi ta gusta Señora hopi.' ('I like Señora. I like her very much.')

Maybe I haven't won any souls for the Faith, maybe with adults I'm a bust – but with these children, I rate – and who can say where the victories are. I don't think anyone can ever tell these children about 'ugly Americans' and make them believe it. I would like to believe that a little order – not too much – was brought into their lives and that fine things are appreciated simply because they are fine, not because society says they're fine. Isn't it too bad that I'm not a public relations person for the US Government instead of a PR for the Bahá'í Faith. OOPS, I said that badly! What I mean is that, while these children may never associate me with the Bahá'í Faith – for very little of it has gotten through to them – they must associate me with my country. All of these children go to a Catholic school where they have already been carefully taught about their responsibility to the church, and all religion, to them, is thought of in terms of the Catholic Church. I cannot tamper with that. I have not the vocabulary nor the skill to teach them of the Faith and I feel it is better not to confuse them. I know the day will come on Bonaire when there will be many Bahá'ís and perhaps, in that day, these children may remember the books and the pictures in the house of the Señora. Maybe enough of the love I feel for them and show them will remain in their hearts so that a greater love can find its way there. I can honestly say that I do not love them because I want them to be Bahá'ís. I love them because I love them, because they are the purest symbols of God's love and because they evoke love within me. What better reason is there to love?

I hope you can see the little girl named Jacqueline and love her as I do.

September 7

This month and probably next month will be the roughest, weather-wise. It is almost unbearably hot and wet. There have been beautiful, wild rain storms almost every night and several times during the day. Today I got caught in one. I had gone to the *playa* as usual in the morning. I went early because although it had stormed violently during the night and I couldn't imagine there could be any more rain up there, it nevertheless did seem clouded over and I thought that if I left early I would return before any more rain fell. Well, you know the story about the best-laid plans of mice, etc. I stopped at the post office and found an empty box which did more than the rain could do – my spirit, not my body, was dampened.

All I needed from the supermarket was cat food. With that tucked under my arm, I stopped to see Carlos. Yesterday, when I saw him, it occured to me that he is not sick. He sits all day in a chair, playing with the ball I got him. He is regaining the use of his fingers and is almost able to move his hand. Everyone is delighted with his progress but I thought, also, of his inactivity. This very active old man is confined to an outdoor corridor in an old-folks home, sitting day after day waiting for visitors – the very thought is distasteful to me. I asked the head nurse to consult the doctor and see if it would be possible for someone with a car to take him for a drive. No one had even thought of that. The doctor said it would be great. Now why in heaven's name didn't the doctor suggest that himself, if he thought it was so great? I communicated this to Carlos' family – now let's see what will happen. I got the head nurse so enthused about his going out that she said if his family didn't take him out, she would.

I've been making discoveries about the Bonairians. Isn't it strange that we never really know all about anyone – or any one people? I have discovered that they simply cannot say 'No'. I wish I had become aware of this sooner. It might have prevented me from counting so strongly on the promises to call on me which were never kept. 'No' is the cruelest word a Bonairian thinks he can say to you. Rather than hurt you with 'no' he says, 'yes' – knowing all the while that he means 'perhaps' or 'maybe' or even 'no'. The only exception has been Raphael who simply says when you try to pin him down, 'I don't promise anything'. Even the taxi men – whose living depends on keeping appointments – don't. I've waited hours for a taxi to show up. I've written messages and taped them on the dashboard of a taxi as a reminder – with the willing consent of the driver of course – only to have him forget. Oh well, I did say this was a relaxed way of life and that these beautiful people took life very easily. Anyway, I love them and will accept them as they are. It does help to understand, though.

I finally got up enough courage to challenge the bill the hospital gave me and, miracle of miracles, the cashier admitted it was rather high and cut it right in half, charging me only 10 guilders instead of the original 20. Can you imagine this happening in the States?

I have discovered that Mr Goilo, the author of the Papiamentu textbook, has been dead for years. The book was written in the 1950s and has been revised several times but there was never a vocabulary list added. I have decided to give a copy of my list, which is almost completed, to the Bahá'ís on Curaçao and let them do with it whatever they think is necessary.

I started to tell about getting caught in the storm. I stayed with Carlos longer than I had planned but decided to try to walk back home in spite of the darkening sky. I have been feeling so great that I often walk both ways instead of taxi-ing back. I got about five minutes from my house when it really came down. Fortunately I had cleared the cemetery and was in the vicinity of some houses. I made a dash for the one that offered a well-roofed porch and asked for permission to stay there. I was very graciously received and found a young woman – a Dutch gal – who spoke very creditable English. We exchanged small-talk for a little while and I found a way to tell her why I was on Bonaire and was able to give her a paper on the Faith, written in Dutch.

This morning about 6:30 every cloud in the sky gathered over little Bonaire and opened up. It is rather difficult to be niggardly and petty in the face of such munificence and generosity as is lavished by nature in this area. When the sun shines, it shines mightily. When the rain falls, it falls abundantly. When the west wind visits, you know it; while the east wind blows, you are lovingly and generously caressed. There is such an abundance of natural things: not just a few lizards but thousands, not just a few kinds of birds but enough to stagger the imagination. Is it any wonder that people raised in such extravagance should be generous, warm-hearted and indulgent?

I had hoped to go again to the beach – every day last week I made arrangements to go – but every day we had rain or the threat of rain. I'm beginning to get stir-crazy. I can't invent enough things to do around the house to keep me busy. It's even harder now because Jacqueline comes in early on Saturdays and Sundays and insists on doing things for me that I would love to do for myself like sweeping the floors, taking out the garbage, washing the dishes. She cannot believe that I would rather do it myself and, since her doing it is an act of love, what can I do but submit?

Mrs Reed has not been very well. Last week I took the boys to the beach with me. That was on Tuesday, the only day weather permitted. We had planned to stay until 5:00 and had arrived at 2:00. At 3:30 I saw the boys with their heads together, seemingly conspiring. I went to them and Neville, the older one, motioned me to go away. Since he had his arm around Evers in a most protective way, I became suspicious. As I approached them they ran out on the beach. It didn't take me very long to discover the problem because the sand was turning red with the blood gushing from Evers' foot.

He had stepped on something in the water and had cut his foot. It was pretty bad. I wish that at this point I could say how resourceful and calm I was, but the truth is, I wasn't. I was panic-stricken! I knew how protective Mrs Reed is of the boys and I dreaded the scene that I felt might ensue when she had to be informed. My panic, then, was not for poor little Evers but for myself.

I had joined a group of women from the Trans World Radio and among them was a registered nurse. She took over at once and declared that the cut was so deep that it would require stitching but that first it would be necessary to have the mother's permission. You see, they all know Mrs Reed. We applied pressure while the nurse got her car and we packed the boys into it. I couldn't go with them because I was expecting my taxi to return for us and there would have been no way to let him know what had happened. It worked out very well. Mrs Reed has a great deal of respect – mingled with awe – for this nurse who is a very large woman with a most forceful personality. She was able to handle the situation very easily and there was no fuss when they went to the doctor's office. Doctor said it wouldn't be necessary to stitch, that pressure bandages would do, that Evers should stay off of the foot for a couple of days. He gave Mrs Reed some tranquilizers and some other medicine for whatever it was that was ailing her and told her to rest in bed too. I wasn't able to see them on Wednesday because of heavy rain but when I went on Thursday the boy was doing very well although Mrs Reed was still not too well. She said they had run out of food and so I offered to do her shopping. She gave me a shopping list that would feed a regiment and on Friday I shopped for her. They live in Noord Nikiboko and I live in Antriol.

The only way we can reach each other is on foot – a walk of about 40 minutes – or by taxi. I used the taxi and made several trips. I think they are all right today although when I saw them yesterday Neville, the older, seemed to have some fever. I told you that there is an over-abundance of everything here.

Just as I love the sun when it hurls its fiery message down to earth, so I love the sudden violent rains which leave behind the healing balm for the torturous burns. Who could score the symphony of wind and rain that beats against my dulled and silenced ear-drums? Secure in the stillness of my house, all my senses are stirred and awakened by the divine music of the tropical storm. Perfumes released from the hot, heavy breast of the earth, ballets performed by trees and shrubs, temple bells ring as drop after heavy drop beats on the tiled roof, timpanies and basses resound deep inside my soul as the unabating fury of the storm continues. How I long to be free and uninhibited – and isolated – so that I could run naked and offer myself to such majesty!

It is late afternoon – an afternoon that was to have been spent at the beach. About half an hour before I was to leave the storm came up and I have been reveling in it for hours. The rain is being blown in through my living-room door – but I could no more close that door on the rain than refuse admittance to a dear and welcome lover. The consequences of the open door will be slight – a wet floor that can be mopped up, a small rug that can be sun dried – but the consequences of a closed door! I won't even think of shutting out such beauty and wonder. Even as I type and watch the rain patterns, I am moved to marvel and to wonder at such generosity, such an outpouring of grace.

My heart has been warmed and uplifted by a letter from the National Spiritual Assembly of Venezuela. I enclose a copy, as well as my reply:

August 25, 1975

Dear Bahá'í Friend,

The National Spiritual Assembly was very pleased to receive your postcard and said special prayers on your behalf at its meeting on July 27th.

You are performing a very important service to the Faith by your efforts in Bonaire and the National Spiritual Assembly of Venezuela stands ready to help you in any way it can. We hope you will keep us informed about your activities and about the progress of the Faith on that small but very important island. We look forward to hearing from you soon.

With warm Bahá'í love,

Asamblea Espiritual Nacional
de los Bahá'ís de Venezuela

Weldon E. Woodard
Secretario

September 3, 1975

National Spiritual Assembly of the Bahá'ís of Venezuela

Dearly-beloved Friends,

Thank you for taking the time to write and encourage me at this post on Bonaire. It is heartwarming to know that you feel my puny efforts are 'an important service'. That I feel very inadequate indeed is saying the very least. I have already made a strong recommendation to both the National Pioneering Committee of Venezuela and the Regional Teaching Committee for the ABC Islands about the teaching work here.

I feel inadequate because I feel that all I am doing is 'holding down a post' and while I am sure there is some need for that and some wisdom in it, it can hardly be dignified with the word 'teaching'. The problem, as I am sure you are aware, is language. Proficiency in either Dutch or Papiamentu is absolutely necessary in order to get the deepest meaning of our Faith across. No tourist-type language can 'sell' the Message. I have made many friends here, as has Rhoda Vaughn, and we are loved and respected, but when I try to make the glories and the wonder of the Message of Bahá'u'lláh known, I find I am unable to communicate. One certainly needs more than 'Macha danki' and 'Mi ta bai playa' to give a spiritual message meaning. I hope I am making my point clear. I have learned a lot of Papiamentu in the time I have been here and I am able to make myself understood but it will take me two or three years to be able to say what has to be said so that these beautiful people will want it.

My recommendation was this: if a Dutch-speaking couple, preferably with school-age children, could be found who would settle here, that would be the answer. School teachers come from Holland with two- and three-year contracts. There are many schools here and I understand that teachers are constantly coming and going. Everyone, except the very little ones and possibly the very old, speaks Dutch. It is the official language and the only one spoken in the schools. Children open doors that others cannot, which is why I suggest a family with children. This is a wonderful place to raise children. Bahá'ís have taken children to awful places to serve the Faith – this place is as close to heaven as one will get on earth. Surely this alone should sell some young couple on the idea.

Also I have suggested that, if at all possible, Mr Gerrit Vernhout of Holland, who did such an outstanding job for the Faith on Aruba, be brought to Bonaire during the Christmas school vacation. He and his wife are willing to come at that time. He is a teacher and if he could be persuaded to think of the ABC Islands as a possible pioneer post I know there would be assemblies all over the place before the end of the Five Year Plan.

As for my work here – it is nothing and has produced nothing. I am merely occupying a house until Mrs Vaughn returns.

I am sorry that this letter isn't more glowing and positive and full of the wonderful things I am doing. I think I am serving you best by my most objective critique.

With deepest Bahá'í love,

Marion West

September 14
5:10 p.m.

ALL week has been singularly lack-lustre. I have spent most of it finishing my vocabulary list for the Papiamentu textbook. I have been on the beach every day but today and it has been wonderful. I have been going at 1:00 p.m. and returning at 5:00. I have made many friends there and have had many opportunities to tell a little about the Faith – which has helped me justify enjoying myself so very much.

During the week, on one of my shopping excursions (groceries, that is), I met a dear little old lady who was completely disoriented and lost. She hesitantly asked me if I spoke English and could I direct her to the Flamingo

Beach Hotel? I could, I did and I seemed to run into her every day thereafter, always lost and bewildered. It became almost a game between us to see where we would find one another. Yesterday, Saturday, she asked me to stop and have coffee with her at a little café. We talked and I learned that she is British, was married to a Pole, a civil engineer stationed in Venezuela who died eight years ago, that she worked as a private secretary to the Canadian Consul-General in Caracas and was now retired and spending her time traveling. It was her first trip to Bonaire and, like everyone else, she had fallen in love with the island. I told her what I was doing on the island and we got into a wonderful discussion on religion and ethical values. She is open-minded and clear-thinking. We became warm and empathetic friends in a very short time. Thank God, this has helped me to see that I haven't lost my ability to communicate when the channels of communication are open, and that I can still 'get through'. She is reading the literature and is eager to contact the Bahá'ís in Caracas. She invited me to spend this day (Sunday) with her at the Flamingo Beach and I eagerly accepted. I had to make the time conditional upon my return from a trip that the Reeds planned and that I had been looking forward to.

Mr Reed works for a company called Chicago Bridge which has been building storage tanks on the northern part of the island for Shell Oil. The job is nearing completion. They figure that it will be completed in January and Mr Reed wanted his wife and family to see the site. They had asked me to go. Early this morning they came for me and we drove out on the island. I wish I had the technical know-how to tell you what I saw. My eyes gathered it all in and I asked lots of questions but my non-technical brain refuses to sort it all out. I can tell you that there are twelve huge tanks and six smaller tanks. We drove around inside the base of one of the smaller ones and it certainly didn't seem very small to me. It was larger than any football stadium I have ever seen and when completed it will be about twelve stories high. I saw how the oil is pumped into the tanks through huge pipelines which are run from the freighters (tankers). I saw how the roof or the top of the tank is raised as the oil flows into it. I saw the pier that the tankers dock at and it scared the heart out of me – so much metal – so monstrous – so mechanized – so soulless! I saw the big crane that Dee Reed operates and felt a great surge of respect and gratitude that there are men who can and will do such work. As Dee spoke of 'his crane' he made you feel that it was a sentient thing, that it actually could respond to his will. I wanted to enter that world with him – because he made it seem as if being in that monster was being in a different world – but I simply couldn't. I tried to personalize that crane as he did but it remained a steel and iron monster and I didn't feel romantic at all about it. I know the men at the site get very good pay and I shall never question their right to it. I wonder if I could ever be married to a man, no matter how much money he made, who could be content with that work. But I'm grateful as I can be for the people in the world who undertake such work.

We had a wonderful drive after we left the site. We drove to the old village of Rincón which was the original slave village in the early days of salt-panning. It was to this little village in the middle of the island, away from everything beautiful, that the men slaves would return on the weekend – after living in the cunucu huts all week on the job. It was there that they had their families. They had no transportation from the 'pans' and it took six hours to walk. It is a very poor-looking little place but the people who live there now love it and feel great pride in it. It has not been tainted by tourism. Not far from the village is a little grotto which is completely open and out of doors – a Catholic place of prayer – in which I felt a great sense of peace. It was just about mid-day when we got there and it was there where I said the noon-day prayer:

> I bear witness, O my God, that Thou hast created me to know Thee and to worship Thee. I testify, at this moment, to my powerlessness and to Thy might, to my poverty and to Thy wealth.
>
> There is none other God but Thee, the Help in Peril, the Self-Subsisting.
>
> *Bahá'u'lláh*

Here I felt closer to the realm of the spirit than in any of the fine churches I have visited. I hope the slides I took reflect the loveliness of it.

My trip with the Reeds was over, and they dropped me off at the Flamingo Beach Club in time for lunch with my new friend whose name is – hold your hat – Tommy Atkins Antonczyk. I told you she was British and how much more British can you get than 'Tommy Atkins'? We had a great time together talking good, satisfying talk. I came alive again. I also met the two new and very young managers of the Flamingo Beach Club. They are Americans, both of them, from upper New York State but both have lived in California and know about the Bahá'í Faith. Oh, it was a bonanza day for me. But alas and alas again, I still have to meet the Bonairian I can talk to at such a level.

It has been a wonderful day. I must find a way to keep the glow with me. I dare not sink into any more fits of despondency. I hope I have it licked – the key seems to be activity. Really, after all, three months of sitting quietly and meditatively should last me a lifetime.

Tomorrow morning at 6:00 I am going to a place called Lagoen. An American friend of Mrs Pieters, my landlady when I first arrived, goes there every morning to fish. He seldom catches anything but insists that it is a divine place just to sit. I am taking a book and a pad and pencil with me and I promised not to breathe a word while he fishes. That will take care of three hours in the morning. I'm always up at 6:00 anyway. Then I will go to the *playa* to see Carlos and go to the post office. That finishes two more hours. At 1:00 p.m. I go to the beach until 5:00 and after that I don't really care. In my next installment I'll tell you about what happened when I took Jacqueline to the beach with me and the Reed boys on Saturday.

September 16
6:50 a.m.

SUDDENLY there is so much to tell that I find it difficult to sort things out. Everything has been happening at once and I can't establish any priority in reporting it so I'll just have to let it flow and come out of the machine the way it wants to.

I've been getting out of bed and dressing very early these past two days because I have been expecting Mr Thomas to come by and take me to the Lagoen. He is American from one of the eastern seaboard states – Massachusetts, I think – who lives a great deal of the year on Bonaire. He and his wife have a house which they keep all year and I doubt if they are off the island more than a couple of months at a time. He seems to be quite wealthy – owns several different kinds of business. I learned, the last time I saw him, that he has a franchise for a cross-country bus line and also a freight line. I met him and his wife while I was living at Mrs Pieters'. Mrs

Thomas has had breast cancer and has had one breast removed. She is a very courageous and strong woman who has made a marvelous adjustment to life but who, unfortunately, does not share her husband's love of the island and the island ways.

I promised to tell you about the day I took Jacqueline to the beach. I had asked her if she swam and she said that she did. I asked her if she had a bathing suit – she didn't. I told her to ask her mother if I could take her with me and that, if I could, I would buy her a swim-suit. Yes, to all of this. It was fun shopping for the suit because the shops where I might find a cheap suit were the shops where only Papiamentu is spoken. The tourist shops where English is spoken are the expensive ones and I didn't dare go to those. Shopping for so specific an item means, of course, asking for it by name – I doubt if the most skilled charadist could act out a 'bathing suit for a twelve-year-old girl'! Well, my Papiamentu was equal to the job and I was able to get just what I wanted. When Jacqueline is pleased, she squeals. There is no other word to describe the sounds that come from her – they are squeals! When I showed her the swim-suit, her eyes opened big and round; her eyebrows almost disappeared into her hairline and she squealed. When she tried it on and saw herself in the mirror, she squealed.

When I got her to the beach she was too embarrassed to take off her dress. I had stopped by to pick up the Reed boys and the shyness between her and them was heavy. I practically had to undress her and pull her into the water with me. BUT when she got into the water, the squealing started. She was like a little wild thing – completely without fear – jumping up and down, squealing and crying out, BUT NOT swimming. I understood quickly that she could not swim. Here again you see the inability of these people to say 'no'. She watched what the boys were doing. They have learned to swim a little and are also without fear. She watched them and then threw herself down in the water – about six inches of water – and began to make swimming motions like the boys were doing farther out. She flayed her arms about and kicked her legs – and squealed and squealed and squealed. Pretty soon she saw that some of the children – even very little ones – were jumping off a pier and she ran to join them. At one end of the pier the water is about a foot deep. At the other end the water is about six feet deep. The smaller children were quite happy to jump off the shallow end and I encouraged Jacqueline to try it. She wasn't too sure and she'd walk to the edge and look down. Then she backed away and seemed to take a running position as if to run the length of the pier before jumping into the water. She ran fine but balked just short of the end. It was so funny to watch her. She got up a good head of steam then put on the brakes – hard – at the edge of the runway. Each time a look of surprise came over her face as she realized that she hadn't made it. Finally, with what must have taken a great deal of courage and determination, she did jump. Of course, she landed in water no higher than her calves but the squeals of delight and the shouting of, 'Señora, bo a mira?' ('Did you see?') were delicious. There is no other word that I can come up with. Her joy and delight were so tangible that I could actually savor them. By this time – that is, after she had jumped from there several times – she had too much confidence and I had to scold her to keep her from jumping in at the deep end. She didn't like that very much and sulked for awhile. I think this was the first time she had been in that beautiful sea that surrounds her island. It was quite a day for me and, although I have been spending four hours every day at the beach, these four hours seemed endless. I was so conscious of my responsibility for three children who didn't belong to me. You remember what happened the last time I took the little Reed boys to the beach!

September 20
10:30 a.m.

It has been several days since I began this chapter and all those thoughts that were coming so fast have flown away. On Tuesday when I picked up my mail there was a letter from the Regional Teaching Committee of the ABC Islands asking me to make some copies of the course on Group Teaching for use on Aruba and to travel there to present it. They were very enthusiastic about the course material and felt that it was just what Aruba needed. I had qualms about using it out of the States because it had been prepared at the request of the National Teaching Committee of the United States. But I reasoned that if I were to try to prepare a course just for the Aruba Bahá'ís it would probably be just like the one I already had – and anyway, what difference did it make where my teaching was done? Wasn't this one Faith all over the world and wasn't the need the same everywhere? I still do feel that it shouldn't be used in the US without the permission of the NTC since, in a sense, if they decide to use it for deepening groups, it is their property. So since receiving this letter, all week when I've been home I've been at this machine making extra copies of the course for Aruba. I still haven't learned when I'm going but I'd better be ready if the call comes quickly.

Now, let me try to pick up the thread.

The big excitement on the island is the arrival of the first oil tanker for the newly-built oil tanks. This was a Dutch freighter but the tug boats that were needed to guide it into the dock at the site came from the US and had to be repainted before they were permitted to 'tug' the big ship. They were sparkling clean and new, a sandy gold color when they arrived; but since the Dutch company's colors are red and dark gold, they had to waste two days repainting the two tugs. I was shocked at the waste of time and money but, evidently, there is some kind of unwritten sea law about the whole thing. The two tugs were named *Ellen McAllister* and *Katherine McAllister* and I wondered how the Dutch were reconciled to that.

I sat on the pier for many hours watching the tugs maneuver. They made many trips to and from the 'site' on the northern end of the island and it was exciting to watch them. But just imagine – if you possibly can – Marion West sitting for hours doing nothing but watching tug boats! 'Mimi' West has no trouble at all just sitting and watching and dreaming! I'm very glad to have discovered her. On the day the big freighter arrived all Bonaire, it seemed, came to Kralendijk to welcome it. All you heard that day was talk of the big ship. Of course, the new storage terminal has created jobs for the island people and will continue to do so as more of the tanks are filled. I am so glad I had a chance to see the 'site' before the filling began. Now I can understand what is happening there.

While I sat at the pier I had a chance to see how the fishermen work – at least some of them. In a small boat – a rowboat, really, equipped with an outboard motor – were three men. One sat at each end of the boat and in the middle sat a man in bathing trunks. He was wearing an underwater mask like the one I wore when Capt Don was teaching me to snorkle. I watched in fascination as I saw him bend over the boat and put his face in the water while the two others, handling oars, guided the boat from place to place in response to signals from the masked man's hands. I realized that he was looking for fish and how very sensible that was. All this was happening right in the harbor before my eyes. After awhile he made a special signal and a huge net was lowered very gently over the side. I didn't stay long enough to see if they caught anything but my guess would be that they did. They seemed too expert to be wasting time. Anyway the sight of wriggly, gasping fish couldn't have been a pleasant one – not one I would have enjoyed.

This morning Mr Thomas did come for me. At about 6:20 a.m. I heard a honk and, sure enough, there he was. I hadn't expected him any more but I was up – how could I sleep past 5:30 when my kitties were clamoring for breakfast? So I was up and toileted but not fully dressed and breakfasted. However I was in his car about three minutes after the honk. It was not quite light but there was the promise of a beautiful day ahead. We drove straight east to the Lagoen and Mr Thomas was right – it was the prettiest part of the island.

After about a ten-minute drive – remember what I told you about the size of the island, only about five miles wide? – we came to a beautiful rough bay. There were no beaches. On three sides there were cliffs and it was a very rugged, unspoiled place, mystically beautiful. The sun was just coming up and there was a hushed, church-like feeling about. The waves in this bay were strong and wild and the sound they made was almost like a huge organ. I took several pictures as soon as there was light enough. There was a concrete pier out into the water and it was onto this that Mr Thomas drove the car. He organized his fishing gear and I went for a walk.

I found myself entirely lifted away from the world. I did some of the best praying I've done here in this wild, natural place. It was so untouched, so unpolluted, so primordial. It was genesis. Time ceased to exist so I don't know how long I walked and sat by the shore. I do know that I felt cleansed and purified and that prayer took on a new meaning. I felt that the word 'transcendent' finally had reality for me. I felt so good and free and not at all like a 'broken-winged bird'. Indeed, I felt that I could soar and fly and outdo Jonathan Seagull himself. I imagine that the Lagoen had much the same effect on Mr Thomas because neither of us talked on the way home. The silence was good and comforting.

We didn't stay there very long because Mr Thomas ran out of bait. He was using soldier crabs and I learned a very interesting thing about them – after I got over the fright of discovering that they had been at my feet all the while we were driving. It seems these little fellows have very little natural protection – they are quite small – so they look for and find shells that other sea things have discarded and live in those. They use one particular shell and I have a couple of them to show when I get back. I was back home at 8:00 a.m. and had so much vigor that I proceeded to tear the house apart and do a thorough house cleaning. I have decided not to go to the beach today but to stay here and get on with all the typing I have to do.

Going to the beach, even though it is expensive because I must taxi there and back, is giving me many wonderful opportunities to speak of the Faith. I think the one most pleasant of these was being able to talk at some length and with much depth to a Mrs Brado, an American lady whose husband is on the Shell Oil tank site project. He doesn't work for Shell. I really don't understand the qualifications of many of the men who are supervising the project, but I think they may be engineers or consultants. Anyway, Mr Brado is being sent to Iran next and they will be there for one year. They are an older couple and she travels with him wherever he goes. I had seen her many times at the beach and we had nodded and smiled but never spoken. She stopped me in the street this week and said she just had to talk to me. She wanted to know who I was and what I did. She said she had been drawn to me because I 'glowed', that she had wanted to speak to me many times but had been shy about it. She said she just felt I had a 'secret' and that she very much wanted to know what it was. Well, she asked for it, didn't she?

She suggested she drive me home and, of course, I accepted. I told her why I was on the island and told her about Bahá'u'lláh and the Faith. She said she had been raised in the Christian Science Church but that she found it sterile and no longer satisfying. I gave her some literature and suggested that, while it might not be politic to look for Bahá'ís in Iran, if she ran into them she would find them gracious and warm and to take advantage of any opportunity to learn more about the

Faith from them. I think I'll have at least one or more chances to talk to her before they leave.

Another exciting thing that happened was that I got to know Capt Don better. He, too, asked me what magic I had that made me seem to be the happiest person on the beach. I told him he had been exposed to the 'secret' but that he hadn't done anything about it.

'Oh, do you mean the Bahá'í Faith?' he asked. 'Is that what does it?'

Then he told me that his very best friend had become a Bahá'í – that he, the friend, had been an avowed atheist but that the Faith 'got him'. When I asked him who the friend was, he told me, 'Hugh Lineberger'.

After talking to Don for awhile he said, 'Hey, I better not talk to you too much. You'll have me convinced. I could never understand what Hugh saw in this but you could sell me.'

Now let me tell you about my dear Carlos. He has almost recovered full use of his right hand. He is a miracle – there is no other way to say it. I don't mean a miracle in the sticky superstitious sense. He is a miracle of the power of the mind to control the body. He simply refuses to be a cripple and he gets a kick out of surprising everyone. He'll sit with that right hand in his lap – looking useless – and then he'll begin to use it. If you watch his eyes you can see the twinkle in them. When he shakes your hand with his right hand he squeezes so hard it hurts and he is delighted. Oh, what a wonderful old man! He tells me that he is trying to move his toes and his right foot. I'll bet he does, although up to now he hasn't had much luck.

I asked him if he thinks of going home.

'No, I never think about that. I'm not unhappy here.

As far as I'm concerned, it's from here to the grave.'

Now with someone else, that would sound morbid, but with Carlos it's just another sign of his good sense.

One of my neighbors gave me a jar of tamarind jam. The very name gets me excited. It's so exotic. If it tasted awful I think I would like it because of its name – but it tastes like heaven. It is tart and sweet; puckery and yet soothing. It is so good! Tamarind trees grow wild all over the place and I have seen the pods fall to the ground but had no idea that the pods had fruit in them. The pods look like big bean pods but are brown and dry looking. Inside are brown seeds covered with a prune-like pulp. The seeds are removed from the pods and simply cooked with sugar. You have to take care eating the jam because all the seeds are still there. The seeds are about the size of a dime.

I also learned about a plant that grows outside my door that can be used to heal rashes and burns. It's a pretty little plant with tiny purple flowers. Louie Martis showed me where to break it off so that the sap would run. This is applied to the troubled area and, like magic, it heals. Is my education being rounded out? I'll say so!

September 23
3:00 p.m.

I'M trying to write this while I sit in luxurious comfort at the beach. It has been said that it takes a cold attic and a scant larder to produce creativity so I guess mine is a lost cause. This kind of luxury is not for struggling artists.

Until just a few minutes ago the scene before my eyes was of serenity, peace and gentle splendor. While I was assembling my writing materials a horde of young ones – like a school of little fish – came out of nowhere and are now disporting themselves gleefully, noisily and aggressively in the sea immediately in front of me. They are of every color imaginable in the human race. I see one little boy whose hair is so light as to be white and – on the other end of the color scale – a kinky, woolly-headed little boy whose skin glistens in the sun like polished ebony. I count fourteen children and all are as much at home in the sea as if they were born in it . . .

I find it's difficult to keep my mind on the writing. They are so cute and so beautiful, I can't take my eyes off them.

Later

I SPENT all weekend at home at the typewriter working on the course I'm going to be giving on Aruba. I didn't try to walk to *playa* and therefore I didn't see Carlos. When I stopped on Monday he was concerned.

'Hey, I missed you. Are you all right?'

I explained that I had been busy.

'You get so many visitors on Saturdays and Sundays, I didn't think you'd miss me.'

'Oh, yes,' he replied. 'When you don't come, I miss you. I like it when you come.'

And, of course, that means that I'm not going to miss any more weekends if I can help it – except when I'm off the island.

I learned some more fascinating facts about this island. For instance, the first Ecological Conference of the Caribbean will be held here this year. There is very much concern about the pollution of the seas and although this part of the Caribbean has suffered very little damage, it is inevitable that it will unless strong and immediate measures are taken to prevent it. Bonaire is especially concerned because its coral reefs are among the finest in the world and in order for coral to survive it must have perfect ecological balance. Below the surface of the water are literally forests of coral and sea vegetation. They require just the right amount of sunlight, air and nutrients to grow and thrive. I haven't enough courage to go down there and look but I've been told, and I've seen pictures to confirm it, that there is a fairyland down there, infinitely more beautiful than anything on land. It is what brings thousands of people here willing to pay big money to enjoy it. I think it costs about US$30 for just one dive. The equipment is terribly expensive and it is reasonable that it should be. One's life depends on the quality of the diving gear. As I sit here I see group after group of 'frog people' – fins, wet-suits, tanks and masks – submerge and not reappear for a long time. Most of them carry expensive underwater movie and still cameras and all reappear with looks on their faces that seem to say 'I've seen another world, another dimension.'

Another thing I learned about Bonaire is that there are only a thousand cars on the island – and no traffic lights. Cars are very expensive. Parts are prohibitive – so everyone learns to take good care of a car. Raphael said he needed a new battery for his car and it would cost about US$130.

Some additional facts about the oil tanker. It's called a 'super-tanker' and is of Norwegian, not Dutch, registry. It carries Nigerian oil, one-and-a-half million gallons of it, enough to fill two-and-a-half of the storage tanks and have some left over to carry to the States. You don't need television when there's something as exciting as a 'super-tanker' on the horizon. Everything stops while the entire population watches it approach. They all watch the maneuvering of the two tugs. They look like two little French poodles (is that right?) frisking around an elephant but they guided that big monster in so gently it was beautiful to watch.

September 24
8:00 a.m.

I'M sure you won't believe this – I'm not sure I do! It happens in comic movies and in silly romantic novels – but, so help me, it happened here. At exactly 4:10 this morning – and the reason I can pin-point the time is that I looked at my watch – I was awakened by what I am sure were drunken voices laughing under my window. There was nothing ominous or frightening about it because it was plainly good-natured and, as I have so often said, I'm simply not afraid. I thought some of the local husbands were coming home after a 'toot' in town and I was prepared to go back to sleep. Oh, no! That wasn't their intention because pretty soon I heard the strumming of a guitar – and darned good strumming it was. Whoever was handling that instrument knew what it was all about. But the singing that accompanied the guitar was right out of *Mad* Magazine. It wasn't to be believed – drunken, off-key, out of tune, maudlin – well, awful is the word. And love songs under my window! I'm still laughing as I type this. It was gosh-darned funny and still is. There must have been three troubadours, each trying to outshout the others. I laughed so long and hard that I was afraid they might hear me. I certainly didn't want my cavaliers to know that I was even aware of them. They sang for more than 20 minutes then got into their car and drove away.

I guess the funniest thing about it was that, although there are three houses close to mine – close enough in case of any trouble – no one from any of the houses made any complaint or gave any sign that they had been disturbed. It was as if it hadn't happened at all. I know some of you who worry about me will see, in this hilariously funny incident, a cause for alarm. That could only be because you don't know these people. I have never felt safer or more secure. If these men were intent on harming me in any way, they certainly wouldn't have advertised their presence with such loud and silly song. All my doors are double-locked – and only because there is no other way to close them. The windows, even when open – as mine are every night – cannot be entered because of the way they are made. So, my concerned loved ones, worry no more. If this had been staged for my benefit, it couldn't have tickled me more. I've really lived! I've been serenaded by troubadours under my window and I bet every one of them was pot-bellied and bald.

I have been asked to serve on the Regional Teaching Committee for the ABC Islands and, although I said I didn't particularly want to be on any committees and that I would serve the Regional Teaching Committee in every way possible without a committee appointment, the National Spiritual Assembly of Venezuela made the appointment and I accepted.

I have completed the typing of the course I'm hoping to do on Aruba. Even with my new-found patience I am eager to have those plans finalized. The Bahá'ís on Aruba must be having difficulties getting together to plan the Institute because it has been several weeks since they were advised of my availability and asked to make plans and inform us. But here is another example of waiting it out and not pushing. I suppose I could go to Aruba and get the whole thing in motion – but then *I* would be doing it and no lasting good would come of it. I have begun to believe that it is sometimes better that something NOT get done than to have to pressure people into doing it. I remember stories about children who didn't learn to speak for years only to have it discovered that their every wish was anticipated and that there was no need for them to ask for anything. When the want or the need was present, they learned to ask. Groups, assemblies, even grown people may be like that: until they feel the need, they will resent your anticipating it. So, hands off, Marion.

Same day
10:40 a.m.

I JUST heard from Carlos that there was nothing either sinister or romantic about my nocturnal serenaders. It seems that it's just an old Spanish custom which is still practiced here when the moon is high and spirits flow. Carlos said that they had most likely been somewhere else before they came here and that, after they left here, they spread their cheer elsewhere. Oh, shucks, another illusion shattered! I thought it was my fatal charm. But it really was funny!

I went to *playa* today just to see Carlos and I'm so glad I did. While I was sitting with him an orderly came by to tell Carlos that they had just brought his sister to the hospital. His sister, the only one he has left, is 80 years old. Carlos lived with her and her family for two and a half years after he returned to Bonaire from the States. He was very fond of her although he didn't quite approve the values of their family. She suffered a stroke just like Carlos about three weeks ago. Her right side, like his, was also completely paralyzed; but, unlike him, she is not making any progress and is unlikely to do so.

She was visiting her son and family on Curaçao when it happened. The doctors there determined that there is nothing they can do for her and they sent her back here to die.

When Carlos was told his sister had just been brought in, he wanted to go over to the hospital at once to see her. I pushed his wheelchair and took him over and up to her room. I knew there had been some coolness between them recently so I was completely unprepared to see my poor Carlos break down as he held her wasted hand and got no response from her at all. He sat at her bedside for awhile and then motioned to me that he wanted to leave. After we left and he had stopped sniffling, we talked. He was so cute.

'Yes, we do have to accept God's Will in everything', he finally admitted, 'but do we have to like it?'

I replied that it wasn't until we learned to like it, that we could truly say, 'I believe', but I had to admit to him that I hadn't really reached that stage yet – and wouldn't it be wonderful when we did? Before I left, he again told me how much my visits mean to him. He has completely regained the use of his right hand and arm. The foot and leg are more difficult but he's trying.

Much later

I HAVE just finished reading a book that has convinced me that I shall never be able to write. Since I've been on Bonaire I've read almost one book a day – and many of them by really good and talented authors – but until I read Ray Bradbury's *Dandelion Wine* I didn't feel envy or a wish to emulate. But his book is the way I want to write. These are the things I would like to be able to say but, in the face of his mastery, I feel so stupid and so untalented. This book is not a science fiction thing. It very simply and exquisitely takes you into the mind of a twelve-year-old boy – but what a boy! He's sensitive, precocious, absolutely natural, positively abnormal – that is to say, he is rare – not like too many other twelve-year-old boys. Bradbury makes me become a twelve-year-old boy and I know, before it happens, what the boy will do and think. I become Douglas and I experience what he does. Now, isn't that masterful writing? There is very little 'story line' – there doesn't have to be. It's just a big chunk of life as lived in the mind of a boy. If I can't learn to write like that, I give up. I'll just have to stop playing with the typewriter and acknowledge how little I know. I know there are better and greater writers than Ray Bradbury but it's his style that I like. If any of you have read *Dandelion Wine*, won't you let me know your thoughts about it? Am I just being weird again? I could have said I'd like to write like Willa Cather or Jessamyn West or a dozen others who can write rings around Bradbury but that's not what I want. I guess I'll just have to be me – and not be a writer.

Sunday noon

THIS is the day I don't like. All the families around me are together and I get that 'all alone' feeling. My mother told me that when I was just a little baby – two years old or so – I used to sit in a little rocking chair and sing, 'All alone – all alone' for long times at a stretch. I wonder if I was liking it or not at that time?

Hugh Lineberger called Don Stewart this week. Don

was very pleased. He told me that Hugh had been best man at his wedding. This got us into another discussion about the Faith!

I really haven't a thought in my head at the moment. I don't even know why I put the sheet in the typewriter for another page. Maybe I just want to see what comes out of nothing!

As I started to say – I feel alone. My eyes go to the door every minute or so, hoping that someone will come although I know that's unreasonable thinking – or wishing. No, that's not quite the way it is because this morning Louie Martis did come for a few minutes – just to see if I'm all right. He and Carlos are very good friends and I almost suspect that Carlos may have told Louie to keep an eye on me since he, Carlos, can't do it. Almost every day, either early in the morning or late afternoon, along comes Louie to check on me. It's very dear and very reassuring to know I'll never again have to lie alone, sick, for four days before anyone knows it.

I'm trying to do a tape of some of the favorite songs that assault the air waves here. I'm trying to get only the 'best' and most popular. I told you that they have a 'hit parade' or the 'best 30' – or whatever they call it in the States. I'm not sure because, at home, I deliberately turned off the set when that came on. However, the music is so much a part of my life here that I want it to keep – like the slides and pictures.

The quality of my tape is not very good but it does capture that eternal, monotonous beat, those really bad voices, the shouting, the sickening, sentimental themes. Someone is always dying of love or for love or because of unrequited love. Oh, I'm not sour on love – far from it – but I'm sour on the whipped-dog kind of begging for love, the asking to be hurt, the sickening need to humiliate oneself. Ugh! Love should make you proud – it should ennoble you, not degrade you. There's nothing wrong with loving where love is not returned. Doesn't God do that so much of the time? That kind of love is not demoralizing. What difference if it is not returned – does that make the loving less? Isn't the wonder and the magic of just loving the best reward of loving?

For some reason, I've been doing a lot of thinking about LOVE. I wish I had someone to talk it over with. I'm not sure if I make sense to myself. I would like to have a sounding board. My thinking goes like this: God's love is constant and unconditional. It doesn't depend on whether or not we love Him. If we love Him, His love enriches us; if we do not respond to His love, we deprive ourselves. He doesn't say, 'Love Me, that I may love thee' – and let it go at that. Rather He says, 'If thou lovest Me not, My love can in no wise reach thee.' That means, to me, that His love is flowing to us but that we block it off by not responding. Now if we could carry that into our human lives, we wouldn't beg for love to be returned. If we love, we love. It's simple. We can't condition that love; we can't turn it off or on. If we love, we love! If the love is returned, lover and loved one are both enriched; if it is not returned, the lover is still a lover. If the love is not returned, that does not make the lover less a lover. At least that's the way I've been thinking and don't ask me why. Tom and I have a very reciprocal love affair. Neither of us suffers from the 'unrequites'. I think it's this constant preoccupation with 'hopeless' love that I hear all around me that has prompted this kind of thinking.

Well, for having nothing to say, I see I've just about filled another page.

I'm trying every trick in the bag to get Tom to take the time and to find the money to come here in December. I want to share with him the beauty and the wonder of Bonaire. Who knows – maybe when retirement time comes we would like to settle here – *Cu Dios ke!* I want everyone to know him and I want him to meet the people with whom my life here has been so closely knit. I want to share this with him – I guess that's the whole of it. If he comes at the end of December, we could go home together. Two weeks here would do him more good – I think – than his chiropractors and his Anaheim Clinic. I don't think my poor love has had a 'vacation' since we've been married. We have always used vacation time to do something for the Faith. He has never, since I've known him, had any time to just relax and do nothing. And I have found that this is not bad. I never thought I would advocate 'doing nothing' and here I am urging it on my love!

October 4

WONDERFUL news to share! Tom is coming to Bonaire! It won't be exactly as I had planned it – but then, what difference does that make – the net results will be the same. Because of the demands of his job, he will not be able to leave the States before January 6th or 7th. Then he will only be able to take two weeks off – which will give him one week on Bonaire, travel time and possibly three or four days to visit my sister and brother-in-law in Georgia. Even one week on Bonaire with as enthusiastic a guide as I shall be should sell him on MY island. I want him to sample this kind of living. Who knows where the Will of God and the needs of the Faith will take us. I want him to KNOW that I don't need city life and the doubtful refinements of 'civilization' in order to be happy. I want him to know that my needs are very simple: I need to teach, I need to love, I need to be clean and I need him. All of that would be here if he were here but I know we would find those minimal requirements in many other places. What a wonderful thing it would be if all prospective pioneers could make a 'trial run'. I would have said that this life was simply not for me if it had been described to me before I came here, and I would have missed the most enriching experiences of my life. Yet if I had to endure squalor and filth and snakes and horrible bugs, maybe I would have found I couldn't take it after all. As I have said before – a Rúḥíyyih Khánum, I'm not! This is very sorry stuff to fashion into a 'pioneer'. Anyway, TOM IS COMING!! I'm making all sorts of plans for that week.

More exciting news! I have just had a letter from the National Spiritual Assembly of Venezuela advising me that they have not only considered my suggestion to bring Mr Gerrit Vernhout and his wife to Bonaire during the Christmas vacation but are actively planning to do so. How I wish Tom and Gerrit could meet. They would love each other so! They are so much alike in so many wonderful ways. Gerrit brings such love with him and such magic – I know all the tender little seeds that have been planted here will flourish in the sunshine of his love and knowledge. I am also bubbling with ideas and plans for his visit. I have written him asking for photos for the newspaper and I'll try to get some good publicity for him. I'll try to arrange a public meeting too. I'm so excited I can hardly type!

My plans for the visit to Aruba have been finalized. I'm leaving here on the 15th of October for Curaçao. I'll celebrate the Feast with them and be on hand for the meeting of the Regional Teaching Committee for the ABC Islands the next day. On the 17th, I'll fly to Aruba and be there for a two-day deepening on Saturday and

Sunday. I've made myself available for whatever they may need for Monday and I'll return to Bonaire on Monday night. Doesn't all this sound like heaven? Here's what I've written to the friends in Aruba and Curaçao.

October 1, 1975

Dear Friends,

I have just made arrangements for my trip to Curaçao and Aruba later this month and I wish to advise you of those plans.

I shall leave Bonaire on Wednesday October 15 at 5:45 p.m. arriving at Curaçao at about 6:00 p.m. It will be a joy to be with the friends in Curaçao for the Feast that night. I shall be available for the Regional Teaching Committee meeting on the 16th and am looking forward to it eagerly. I shall leave Curaçao on Friday October 17 at 2.50 p.m., arriving Aruba at about 3.05 p.m. Because I cannot make proper connections out of Aruba on Sunday night, I can stay over on Monday and be available for any deepening or consultation that the friends there may wish or I can be available to speak with contacts. At any rate I can be used by the Aruba Bahá'ís in any way they see fit to use me. My plan, unless it should be necessary to change it, is to leave Aruba on Monday the 20th at 7.55 p.m. and make a direct flight to Bonaire. I hope these plans suit the arrangements that you are making for my visit; if they do not, there is still time to make changes if you will *quickly* let me know.

I am sure there is no need for me to tell you the importance of this deepening Institute. Its purpose is to prepare the Bahá'ís on Aruba to form one or more Assemblies in accordance with the plan laid down by the Universal House of Justice. This is not a mere whim of the Regional Teaching Committee; it is a vital part of the building of the New World Order to which we are all committed.

I have no doubt that you on Aruba are Bahá'ís in your very hearts; I am sure that I will not have to 'sell' you on the Faith; I have no question of your love and devotion. But I know that there are so many things that you will have to learn about conducting the business of the Faith in an entirely new way – the Bahá'í way – and that is what the course is intended to do. I beg you to make every effort to get all the Bahá'ís that you possibly can to the two-day Conference. It may be necessary to organize car pools to get many of them to the meeting; it may be necessary to make plans to feed everybody; but whatever it takes, it is necessary that ALL be present. The course that I shall give was originally intended to be taught at a summer school for one week but I am condensing it to a two-day course. This means, of course, that it will be intense and that attendance for the whole two days is preferable. However, if some can't be there for the full two days, whatever time they can attend will be better than nothing. I am specially writing this to Mr Buckley and Dr Eerland in the hopes that both of you will be able to round up the others. I cannot tell you with what eager anticipation I look forward to my trip to Aruba.

With deepest Bahá'í love, in His service

Marion West

Carlos' sister died. He felt so sad because, as he kept saying over and over, 'But she was only 80. I'm 86 but she was only 80.' She was buried Thursday. When I went to see him on Tuesday I found the whole family there and learned at once that she had died in the night. I stayed only for a minute and told Carlos I would see him the next day. I didn't feel that I belonged there at that time. When I spoke to him later I found that he had not gone to the funeral. Again his good sense showed itself.

'What good could I have done her?' he said. 'I would have been a problem for the family. They would have had to carry my wheelchair or I would have had to stay outside the gate. I can grieve for her just as much right here.' Then he took my hand and said, 'I want to thank you for leaving the other day. Not everybody would have known that it was a time for just family. Thank you.'

Now have I underestimated his sensitivity or his 'class'? He is a rare old man. I also learned that he has been practicing yoga exercises for years – or had been, at least. His face is unwrinkled and unlined, his back is straight and, before his stroke, he walked miles every day without fatigue. He was very pleased to learn that I am exercising every day and is tickled pink every time I tell him that I walk both ways.

October 9
2:30 p.m.

SUCH excitement! If I can only hold myself down long enough to tell it all! And where to begin! You remember I mentioned the two little tugs that were berthed here at Bonaire for the purpose of guiding the big tankers into the oil terminal, and that their being here was such an event that all Bonaire came to the waterfront to watch them. Well, I got to thinking that, if I knew more about what went on aboard those tugs and understood more of the way they work, I could bring some more of the local color and feel to these letters. On Tuesday night before I went to sleep the plan came to me. On Wednesday I would go to the pier and try to find the captain of one of the tugs and ask him if I could come aboard to ask him some questions – you know, like a reporter.

Well, I did go to the pier and I did go to the tug only to lose my nerve: I simply couldn't carry it through. I saw many fellows working around the boat, scrubbing and polishing, but I couldn't find the voice to ask for the captain. I walked away angry with myself for being such a ninny. I did my shopping, saw Carlos, went to the post office, etc. and went home to wait for Doie (my taxi driver) to pick me up at 1:00 to take me to the Bonaire Beach Club. I had stopped heaping abuse on myself and accepted the fact that for all my 'push' and 'brass', I just didn't have it.

I was enjoying a rare sunny day at the beach. It had rained every day and I was forced to stay at home and was beginning to get a little 'stir-crazy' so the sun and the sea and the sound of English voices, the companionship of the many people I had come to know there, was relaxing and soothing.

It was getting close to the time for Doie to come back for me (5:00 p.m.) when two men appeared on the beach. I had not seen them before but some instinct prompted me to ask if they were from the tug. There was absolutely no visible reason for me to suspect this – just pure hunch. They were the captain and first mate of the 'lead' tug. Although the tugs had been in port for a long time, this was the first time either of the men had come to the Beach Club.

All of the guests at the club gathered around them and began to ask questions and I joined them. When I mentioned that I had been at the pier with the intention of finding the captain and asking permission to come aboard, Capt Richard said that he would be very happy to show me whatever I wanted to see. The mate (Martinus) suggested that I return with them that afternoon. They had come over in a little skiff. I begged off because I knew there would be no way of letting Doie know and, besides, I was a mess – sea water and sand – and wanted to shower and dress.

Martinus asked me if he could take me to dinner and to the movies that night. He said he had not been off the boat since it had come and that he was sick to death of the boat and the company of men. I accepted – I hope not too quickly. I, too, was sick to death of the four walls of my house and my own company, and the thought of a pleasant break was not unwelcome. The plan was that Martinus would come for me at 7:00 p.m. and, after dinner at the Flamingo Beach Club, we would go to the local movie. In the morning the tug was to go to work. Another tanker was due during the night and had to be berthed at the site. Capt Richard invited me to go along and see them at work IF I could be at the pier at 8:00 a.m.

Martinus is a big Dutchman (who hates the Dutch). His mother was Jewish and his father was not. During the occupation of Holland by the Nazis, his father had smuggled Martinus out of Holland to the US where he lived and worked and considered himself an American. He spotted me as a 'landsfrau' at once and was delighted. He told me that he had always identified himself with his 'Jewishness' and wore it 'proudly' – a very interesting man. He is quite a philosopher, very well read – he won't read some of the 'junk' that I will read. He lives in Tampa, Florida, and thinks it's the most wonderful spot on earth. He hates Bonaire because of its Dutchness and said that, if he had known he was being sent to this place, he would have refused to go.

We went to dinner and I found him to be a very cultured, urbane and pleasant dinner partner. When we discovered that there was no movie last night, he suggested that perhaps I would like to come aboard the tug where there were some guests already. In spite of the raised eyebrows that I can almost see, I went and I was perfectly safe and enjoyed a wonderful evening. The wife of one of the officers had come to visit her husband (they live on Aruba) and there were a couple of local people there. They were playing rummy and having lots of fun.

I stayed until about 11:00 and then Martinus got a taxi and took me home. He told me not to eat breakfast, that Capt Richard had invited me to eat on board. On the way home from the Beach Club, earlier in the day, I had told Doie how excited I was about going on the tug while it was working. I was prattling like a child and Doie, who has become a good friend, was very pleased about it. He knew very well how lonesome it has been for me and was happy that I now had something exciting to look forward to. When I told him that I intended to walk to the pier in the morning, he wouldn't hear of it. He said he would come for me at 7:30 and that it would be his gift to me; he wouldn't let me pay him – he just didn't want me to have to rush and to walk.

I was so excited that I barely slept and at 5:00 a.m. I was up. After I fed the cats and did my exercises, I showered and dressed and was waiting for Doie at 7:00 a.m. Fortunately he came early because, when we got to the boat, they were waiting for me and said that if I hadn't come in a few minutes they would have had to leave without me. They had got word that the tanker was hovering near the site – waiting for them – and they had to get going. See, if I had walked and arrived there at 8:00 a.m. as I had planned, I would have missed them.

Getting on board was scary for me. There was no gangplank and I had to jump over the side from the pier. I didn't dare show what a chicken I am so I closed my eyes and followed Martinus' voice and jumped. We went down below where the others were waiting for breakfast – and what a breakfast! I should have known from the girth of the captain that they ate well. Richard is from Louisiana – a Cajun – who likes his food and Martinus had told me that they had the best table of any tug in the McAllister fleet. I had to beg off. My skimpy breakfasts at home had left me unable to cope with such a banquet, but I did do justice to whatever I could eat. As soon as the pilot came on board we were off, *Ellen* in the lead and *Kathryn* following. It was a beautiful morning and, as soon as breakfast was over, Ludwina (the other gal) and I were taken up on the bridge where we spent the entire three and a half hours.

I'll try to let you know and feel what I saw and felt but it won't be easy. First let me say that when the engines began to turn I could feel a power come from them that was incongruous in such a small boat. However once I was aboard I lost the sense of 'smallness'. *Ellen* seemed so big and powerful.

After leaving the deck we proceeded through narrow

passageways like on a submarine and descended a narrow winding ladder-like stairway to the floor below. I know they don't call it a 'floor' and that was one question I forgot to ask. Below was the kitchen, the dining area and a couple of bunk-rooms, as well as a 'head' and the laundry room. There was also a lot of other stuff around that had to do with operations but no one thought it was important to say what they were and I wanted to save my questions for the important stuff. Off the dining area there was another steep winding stairway, almost like a ladder, that led to the upper bunks. Here were the captain's quarters and those of the officers. I had seen them the night before. On that floor also were storerooms.

Another ladder led to the bridge and when – the night before – I had declined to go up that forbidding ladder, I had been told, 'Well, like it or not, that's where you'll be going tomorrow!' so I was prepared and determined not to be a sissy. Up that ladder I went and found myself in a most fascinating place – the bridge or wheelhouse – with all its cockpit-like apparatus. It did indeed look like the cockpit of an airplane. Capt Richard, who had guided the tug out from the pier, relinquished the controls to a beautiful young Bonairian who was being trained as a tug-boat captain. This young boy, Pete, was, like so many Bonairians, blonde of hair with grey-blue eyes but with a wonderful milk chocolate skin. He was a natural seaman. Richard began to explain the various instruments to me and excited me tremendously by telling me how his tug and another had performed a salvage mission on an oil tanker that had struck a reef off the Bahamas and had caught fire. Little *Ellen* had been able to put out the fire and had been able to help rescue 37 of the 41 men on board. They were waiting for salvage pay which Richard said would amount to quite a lot of money for each of the crew.

Everyone had expected me to get seasick and I was so proud to have fooled them all. I not only didn't get seasick but I felt marvelous. The water was so blue and the sky and clouds so beautiful. We could see schools of the graceful flying fish that add such color and glamour to Bonaire.

Pretty soon, on the horizon, we saw the tanker. It had arrived during the night and had 'laid to' until this morning. The water is too deep for them to drop anchor, so they just have to go around in circles waiting for the tugs.

Ship to ship communication began between the *Ellen* and the *Tamamba* (the tanker) and, as I watched, that big ship began to come toward us. The closer it got, the bigger it got and I recalled what I had said about poodles and the elephant. It still held! The pilot was on our boat and we were supposed to get him on the *Tamamba* – how, I couldn't imagine. She was so high above us; we were like minnows playing around a whale. (Hey, I found a better simile!) As I watched, I saw a rope ladder being played out from the Tamamba. Straight down the gigantic side came this snake-like rope as Capt Richard nudged the *Ellen* close to the big one's side. I understood now why there were heavy rubber bumpers at the front of the *Ellen*.

Ellen nosed right up to the tanker and then slowly turned so that her side was hugging the big one. From down below I watched the pilot, as agilely as a monkey, jump from the deck of the *Ellen* to that swaying, swinging, rope ladder and begin the climb up, hand over hand. My heart was in my mouth until I saw hands reach over the side of the tanker and pull him aboard. He waved us off and, as skillfully as she had clung to the *Tamamba*'s side, *Ellen* pulled away with not even a tilt or a sway. It was the most beautiful thing I had witnessed.

All this while two tiny little yellow boats were approaching and I was told they were 'line-boats'. When I asked what they did, Richard said, 'Wait and see'. With the pilot guiding it, the tanker made for the terminal dock. It had taken about 40 minutes to make the rendezvous with the *Tamamba* and about 10 minutes to get the pilot on her deck. Now we made a slow approach to the terminal where the tugs' work would really begin. With the *Ellen* in front and the *Kathryn* behind and guided by the pilot, huge lines were tossed up to the tanker from the tugs. The first of these lines was a nylon one tossed up by young Pete to the waiting hands of the *Tamamba* crew, tossed with such deadly accuracy that I couldn't believe what I was seeing. The last rope was a cable about as big around as a man's waist. I think it might help you to see this if you realize that the tanker was at least as high above us as a 10 to 14 storey building would have been! Can you imagine throwing a nylon line – no matter how heavily weighted – that far and that high?

After the two tugs had been secured to the tanker, the push-pull began. For awhile I couldn't understand what was happening because our engines were off. Then I realized that the big ship was, in fact, pulling us and that's what happened until, at an order from the pilot, we started our engines again and we were in business. I shall never cease to marvel at the skill of our captain. All the while the air was alive with telephonic communication – one tug to another, tanker to tug, pilot to terminal – all kinds of exciting talk that I couldn't begin to keep up with.

After about one hour of this kind of stuff, while the two tugs were holding the ship steady, the tow line boats got into the act. From big 'holes' in the tanker came heavy, heavy rope lines. From our side (the port side) I saw three. I was told that on the starboard side at the front (and I know that isn't what it's called) and at both sides at the rear of the tanker three lines were being lowered. The line boats, manned by Bonairians, three to each – a helmsman and two crewmen – had to catch those lines and carry them to platforms out in the sea near the terminal dock. Here they were made secure and were used instead of anchors. The water is too deep for the use of anchors and this is the way the big ships are held fast while the unloading is taking place. All the while the pilot is giving orders to the tanker captain as well as to the captains of both tugs: 'I need ten more feet', 'A little to the starboard', 'Hold it steady', 'Hard around, *Ellen*' etc., and with instant and exact obedience, all orders were executed. An instant's delay would have been hazardous. All this took about two hours. We had left Kralendijk at a little after 7:30 and at almost 11:30 we got the signal to shove off. The *Tamamba* had been secured – our job was done. It was the most breathtaking and exciting thing I had ever witnessed. The chef came up to tell us that dinner would be served as soon as we reached Kralendijk – another 30 to 40 minutes.

We were served a good dinner – roast beef, mashed potatoes and rice and beans and salad, hot rolls (homemade), baked apples and anything to drink that one could ask for. A man-type meal for men who had earned it. Almost as soon as we had finished dinner, I was told that my taxi was here. I hadn't ordered a taxi but dear, dear Doie, who was watching the tugs return, felt I would need a lift and was there. What a morning!

Please DON'T worry about me. As long as I am without fear and my actions and motives are pure, NOTHING can hurt me. You will never know how much I needed this.

October 23
1:00 p.m.

I SEE that it has been a long time since I last wrote and although much has happened, I am having a difficult time sorting things out. As usual, I'll just ramble and see where my thoughts take us.

On the 15th of October I left Bonaire for Curaçao. This time I stayed with Angela Lenderink, the secretary of the local Assembly and the Regional Teaching Committee. Even here secretaries are hard to come by and, often, a good one has to double up. Angela is English, married to a Dutch man. Cappy Lenderink has a fabulous history. He was a captain in the Dutch Navy, commanded a destroyer, did submarine duty, became – after his discharge from the service – a demolition expert and worked after the war on cleaning the Dutch harbors of bombs. He is also a pilot, has his own plane (a four-seater) and practically commutes among the islands. He has a very lucrative business dealing in commercial gases. He also supplies the air for aqualungs and hospital oxygen and stuff.

The Lenderink home is super: air conditioned, elegant, gracious. Angela has two live-in maids, one who does the cooking and one who cleans. It was very plush and I must admit that for me it was a little bit of heaven. My hedonistic instincts reveled in all that luxury. I had a beautiful guest room complete even with an electric mosquito killer. I stayed there from Wednesday till Friday afternoon.

On Wednesday we had the Feast and it was one of the most beautiful Feasts I've had in a long time. Angela is a perfectionist and the Feast showed it. Almost all the Curaçao Bahá'ís were there plus a guest, Dr Eerland from Aruba. On Thursday night the Regional Teaching Committee for the ABC Islands met and we had an election. Thank God, we had enough sense to re-elect Angela as secretary. I am chairman and Nosrat Rabbani is treasurer.

On Friday Angela took me to visit the Synagogue. This was a very moving experience. The Temple Mikve Israel-Emanuel is the oldest in continuous use in the western hemisphere. It was dedicated in 1732 and has always been used. There is a large and very prosperous Jewish community on Curaçao. They fled from Portugal and Spain and are mostly Sephardic Jews. The Temple is exquisite. I have bought colored postcards to show when I get home because my words would fail even to hint at the beauty here. The floor is sand of the whitest, finest kind imaginable. It is almost like a fine talc. It is swept and sifted every day and adds something subtly wonderful and mysterious to the place. They say it is in commemoration of the 40 years in the wilderness and desert but it also has acoustical value. They say it deadens all sounds other than the chanting and praying.

Adjacent to the Temple is a museum and that was a soul-stirring experience for me. It brought back memories of my childhood. I could see my grandmother blessing the Sabbath candles and the Sabbath cholah (bread). I could see my uncles putting on the 'tvillem' (phylacteries). So many memories came rushing over me that it was almost hard to bear. You know, it is true that you can take the Jew out of Judaism but you cannot take the Jewishness out of him or her. The race instinct in a Jew is very strong. I feel that it has very little to do with the religion, really; that it is more a racial instinct than a religious one. Someday I'd like to do some research on this and see where it takes me. I responded very strongly to the Temple and the museum and was very grateful to Angela for taking me there. She says she takes all visitors there. She feels it to be one of the most important things to see on Curaçao. I think 'see' is the wrong word – it is more like 'experience'!

Friday afternoon I flew to Aruba and, from that moment on, I was not too happy. I wish I could write something glowing and wonderful about my visit but from the moment of my arrival everything seemed to go wrong. In the first place my luggage did not come off the plane. It went back to Bonaire – and when they wired Bonaire about it, they were told that it would come on the next plane, four hours later. Secondly, the young man who was to meet me did not show up. I had only one phone number, that of Dr Eerland who is a pediatrician. I reached him at his office to learn that he would be busy seeing patients until late afternoon. I had arrived about 2:55 p.m. He said he would try to reach the young man who was to come for me but that if he couldn't, he would come himself as soon as he could. I waited until about 6:30 and then, in desperation, called his home. His wife, not a Bahá'í, said that he was still at his office but she would come for me. At a little after 7:00, she did. I was not liking Aruba very much by this time. She took me to her home although I was to stay with a non-Bahá'í friend of the Faith. We called Mrs Florence Wekker as soon as I got to the Eerland home and explained why I was so late. The doctor arrived a little later and took me to Mrs Wekker's.

Mrs Wekker is a most unusual and charming woman. I think I'll have to do a sketch on her like the one I did on Jacqueline. She was born in Surinam to a Chinese mother and a black Surinamese. She is dainty and, to me, beautiful. She deplores her 'large mouth' but I think she is a very beautiful woman – as well as a very beautiful person.

Her flat – which she rents – is right in the heart of downtown Oranjestad, Aruba. I couldn't, for the life of me, have said, 'In the heart of BEAUTIFUL downtown Oranjestad', because it is ugly. Her flat is quite nice; it is clean and interestingly furnished. Good taste and money are evident but there was not a sign of a book any place. This made it seem bare to me. My room was very small and very hot and very noisy. The one small window opened on a bar where loud and drunken noises could be heard until dawn.

Florence was very solicitous of my comfort and she offered me, from her heart, the best she had. After seeing the way the rest of the Aruban Bahá'ís lived – with the exception of the doctor – I was thankful that I was staying with her and not them.

I have never seen such poverty in my life. It is so sad because there is so much wealth on Aruba. It is the 'run-away' place of many of the movie people; also the jet-set (whatever that is) uses Aruba. There are magnificent hotels and gambling casinos and very expensive homes. So the awful poverty of the black people is hideous and unbelievable. The heat on Aruba was intense and I developed a heat rash all over my body – from my scalp to my toes – which almost drove me mad. I still have the remains of it and am only just getting it under control. Because of the poverty of the Bahá'ís, they have no autos and transportation is a problem. Dr Eerland has to fetch and carry everyone. It was with difficulty that we gathered six of the friends for a meeting Saturday late afternoon. On Sunday we met from 10:30 a.m. until about 2:30 p.m. and were fortunate to have eight of the believers there, which is a pretty good attendance. I found them to be so undeveloped that I had to cut a lot out of the course which they would have had difficulty understanding. Dr Eerland is doing more than he should or can and it is very difficult for his wife.

But there was a great deal on the positive side too. I was able to get the friends to arrange the next four Feasts, each one at a different house, and I did make it clear that the Eerlands cannot be expected to haul everyone. There is still no clear feeling as to whether they should try to work for two Assemblies or start with one and split when two can be formed. I think it would be a mistake to separate them now.

I had originally left Monday open for private consultation and/or deepening on demand – and had my ticket to return Monday night. No one took me up on that offer so I wanted to go home Sunday night or Monday morning. Florence wouldn't hear of it.

'You have given two days to the Bahá'ís, she said, 'now you can give one day to Florence.'

You know I couldn't refuse that. So I stayed. Florence took me on a tour of the island and it really is a very beautiful place, much greener than either Bonaire or Curaçao. The beaches stretch for miles and are as white as snow – with lofty palm trees shading them – but all of this was spoiled for me by the knowledge of what else existed on the island. Well, we lost track of time and as a result, I missed my plane by about one minute and had to stay over until Tuesday morning. I was hating Aruba more and more every moment even while my good sense was telling me that none of this was Aruba's fault.

When I got home to Bonaire, I could have kissed the ground! I wonder if I could have stuck it out for six or seven months if I had been sent to Aruba or even Curaçao. Thank God and the International Goals Committee for sending me to Bonaire, my beautiful, peaceful gentle Bonaire. My grandmother used to say – and this is a translation from the Yiddish – 'God sends the cold according to your clothes'. Another way of saying He doesn't try you beyond your endurance – and He knows mine is very low.

One of the most spectacular events on Bonaire is currently being held: the Annual Sailing Regatta. While I was at the Lenderinks' the youngest daughter, Brigit, was sad because they were not able to get reservations for her and her girlfriend at any hotel on Bonaire for the event. The family would have let her go if they could have had a place for her to stay, although the child is only fourteen years old. All the Caribbean islands take this event very seriously and there are also entries from many countries in South America. Brigit and her friends are water happy. They sail, boat, dive, scuba and otherwise; they also water-ski. They, like most Antillians, are as much at home on and in the water as on land. The child was so unhappy and the Lenderinks' hospitality so great that I offered floor space as the only thing I had to offer.

It was arranged that Cappy would fly the girls over and that they would bring what they called 'stretcher beds' – a kind of fold-up canvas tent cot – and their own linens, etc. They arrived on Wednesday morning at 10:00 and I had my taxi there to pick them up. I had found a wire from my nephew from Puerto Rico saying that he would arrive on Thursday at 9:30 p.m. It was going to be fun – one bathroom, a shower stall with no door, only two chairs at the dining table, barely enough dishes for two. But I knew we could manage.

I had prepared the girls for very simple living and have been joking with them, since they arrived, that they couldn't imagine such simplicity. Both of these girls are from very rich homes and cannot imagine how or why I can live like this. I think they have a better feel for the Faith since coming here. Brigit, like her sisters, has rejected her mother's Faith and has even put it down, but I think she has more respect for it now. I am trying to make the girls as comfortable as possible, remembering my recent experience on Aruba. I have emptied my dining room of the furniture and turned it into a sleeping room for them.

I was going to give my nephew the storage room, for which I have rented a bed – which I shall keep for Tom. But this morning I had a wire from him saying that he was not coming – he had cracked a rib in an accident. It is not serious, just enough to keep him home. In a way I'm glad he will come later. It would have been hectic and I know he wanted to spend a quiet time with me. The island during the Regatta is like a mad house; beaches are so crowded there is not a place to put yourself. It looks like Coney Island in July. When he comes later, it will be better. So, again, you see how He has a way of taking care of things. Oh, I don't mean He cracked Teddy's ribs so that he could come at a better time – even though that's the way it sounds!

The girls are so sweet, even though I don't think either one of them has ever made her own bed or washed a dish. But you can bet they are doing it here – and not minding it. Their questions about the way I live are so funny.

'But where do you wash your clothes? Where is your machine? Who does your cleaning? Do you *walk* to town?'

They were unable to sleep last night because they are so used to air-conditioning, so tonight I will give them my electric fan. I am, by now, more accustomed to doing without it than they.

I have my ticket for my trip to Caracas, Venezuela. I leave here on the 10th of November and will be there until the 17th. Needless to say, I am looking forward to that trip. In view of what happened on the trip to Aruba, I have written to the National Spiritual Assembly of Venezuela asking them to have me paged by whoever meets me at the airport in Caracas.

I am trying to arrange to stay over in Curaçao for a week before I return to Bonaire. We will have another Regional Teaching Committee meeting and the Local

Spiritual Assembly of Curaçao want me to do a deepening for them. Also I have pretty definite word that Gerrit Vernhout, from Holland, is coming to help me on Bonaire during the Christmas vacation. He will be here for about two weeks. I must arrange for a meeting place, news coverage, personal invitations, a place for him to stay (we have both agreed that he couldn't possibly stay here – it might cause loose talk) and to rent a car for him. The thought of all that activity is so sweet and the knowledge that real and good help is coming is so wonderful. It is enough to take my mind off any unpleasantness. Cysts, heat rash, bugs – all can be dealt with as long as I feel I am serving and working.

October 25
5:00 p.m.

WELL, the Regatta is over and I'm not sorry. I didn't enjoy it very much. The beach was so crowded with noisy, rude, inconsiderate people that there was no pleasure being there at all. I didn't understand what was going on; all announcements over the loud speakers were made in Dutch. I sat for four hours without hearing one word of English. Now I know what it feels like to be a 'foreigner'. Have you ever stopped to consider what people who come from other countries may feel like when they come to the USA without a knowledge of OUR language? It's rough – you know things are going on and you can't participate. It makes you feel stupid. It certainly is deflating and ego-destroying. I think more Americans need that experience.

There were some moments of extreme beauty during the Regatta. There was an event for a little boat called the 'Sunfish'. It is a one-man job with one large sail. Four teams were competing; each team had three boats and each team had a different color sail. One was red and white stripes; another, blue and white; a third, green and white; and the fourth, yellow and white. The twelve little boats all entered at the same time, so I couldn't understand what the competition was about. What I did understand was the exquisite grace and beauty of those dainty things skimming the surface of the water and looking like huge butterflies as they receded into the distance. There also were several – oh gosh, I forget the name of them – I *think*, but I'm not sure, they were called trimaran – anyway there were several of those. They are quite large but surprisingly graceful and it was good to watch them on the water. They had many high-powered speed boats, too, but I didn't like those. I went only one day because I didn't enjoy it very much. I'll be so glad to go tomorrow and find the beach clean again and quiet.

The day I went to pick up the girls at the airport, I found a native Bahá'í – a young man by the name of 'Boochie' Statie. Rhoda Vaughn had given me his name as a Bahá'í but every attempt to locate him had been abortive. He seemed genuinely glad to meet me and promised to visit me after the Regatta. I'll not hold my breath. I've learned that lesson, but at least I know how to get hold of him if I should want to. I asked him if he still considered himself a Bahá'í and he said, 'Yes', but that he didn't have anything to read or study. I assured him that I did have some good things that I would give him. I do have some things in Dutch that I bought when I was on Curaçao; for instance, Gloria Faizi's *The Bahá'í Faith* in Dutch.

I went to the newspaper office in Curaçao. All newspapers that are received on Bonaire are published and printed in Curaçao. I went to put an ad in one of the more popular papers here, the *Amigoe*. I am including the text of the ad material because, while you may not know it, some of you have helped pay for that ad. It was quite expensive but I wanted to try one more dramatic thing and that was what we, the Regional Teaching Committee, came up with. It had to be in English because if it were in Dutch or Papiamentu and there was a response in those I would have been stymied again. If there is a response, at least I will know that it will be one that I can handle in English. If I decide to run another ad, it will be a much smaller one. This one ran for a whole week. It is hard to get used to the ways things work in another culture. Shortly after I got here, I wrote and called the man who handles news and ads for *Amigoe*. He lives on Bonaire and is Dutch. I told him I was planning to run an ad and asked him to come to see me. He never did. I shall have to try him again now that he knows an ad was placed for the Faith. We shall see. Incidentally, his name is one I got from Mr Mázgání as having shown some interest in the faith after Mr Mázgání's public lecture before I arrived.

This is the ad. I'm sure we might have come up with something more original but the entire committee worked on it and it was the joint effort of all. There are many things to consider.

We feel that, if nothing else is accomplished, the word Bahá'í is prominent and the fact there there is an Information Center established. The next ad will be different.

We hope that, having paid for advertising, we might

Amigoe

WOENSDAG 22 OKTOBER 1975

ONE WORLD
– ONE RELIGION –
ONE MANKIND

ARE YOU INTERESTED?
FOR INFORMATION WRITE:

BAHA'I INFORMATION
CENTER
Box 33 – Bonaire
Box 804 – Curaçao

have an easier time getting a good news release when Mr Vernhout comes in December. He has sent me a good glossy photo for the paper which I hope they will use.

I think I would like to make one observation about the people at the Regatta. We Bahá'ís dream of a world where there is no color barrier, where colored skin is considered beautiful. Well, that world was plainly visible here. There were so many cases of mixed-marriages with the resultant beautiful children. It was enough to rejoice any Bahá'í heart. I knew that there had been a lot of inter-marrying in the past – whether those marriages were legal or not – but I hadn't realized that it was still prevailing, legally. Here were happy families, beautifully mixed; some so young, others still not middle-aged, and some much older. In all the groups that clustered together there was a mixture of some kind. That situation may take a long time in the States but it is on its way.

October 31
2:30 p.m.

I'M waiting till it is time to go to the airport to pick up my nephew Teddy who is coming to visit me for a few days from Puerto Rico. I haven't seen him in several years. When he was a little boy, he was as dear to me as my grandson Michael is and I used to take him everywhere with me. Now he is a man and will probably treat me like – well, I don't really know how he'll treat me! I dare him to make an old aunt of me! He teaches at the University at Arecibo, PR. I think his subject is history. I have made sure that everyone knows he is 'mi sobrinu na Puerto Rico' (my nephew from Puerto Rico). I've seen to it that word has been spread around the island so there will be no loose talk. Ted is a man – a big man – and I want his relationship to me clearly defined. Bonaire has the best grapevine communication anywhere; if you sneeze in Antriol, Rincón knows it in minutes. That is the reason that, when I do have men visitors, we sit outside on the porch in full view of all Bonaire – except when it rains when we sit in the living-room with all lights blazing.

I did have a visitor about whom I'm very excited. When I came out here I was given a couple of names of people who were supposedly Bahá'ís. Every effort to find them was fruitless. But finally, as I have already stated, I found one at the airport. His name is Juan Statie – called 'Boochie' – and, although the names are the same, he is not closely related to Raphael Statie. He had promised to visit me and I really didn't expect him, but last night he came and we spent a wonderful couple of hours together.

I asked him why he had become a Bahá'í and he said it was because of the 'Story'. He explained that the story he was told of the suffering of Bahá'u'lláh was enough to convince him that Bahá'u'lláh had a Message that he, Boochie, wanted. He spoke the name 'Bahá'u'lláh' with such love and reverence that there was no doubt in my mind that he knew what he was accepting and Whom. A teacher from Trinidad had been on Bonaire and had given him the Message but had left shortly after, promising to send him books. Unfortunately, the books did not come and he has had only the 'Story' to sustain him in the Faith. He understands English pretty well but does not speak it well. Nevertheless, we managed to have a good deepening session during which he asked me to tell him what the Bahá'í laws were on marriage and sex. He is married and has a little boy. His wife and family are Catholic but he says there will be no problem about his Bahá'í activity. So far, he has told no one that he is a Bahá'í. I was able to give him some books. I had bought a few 'Gloria Faizis' in Dutch, along with several good pamphlets in Dutch, while in Curaçao. I shall bring back some things in Spanish when I return from Caracas next month. At any rate, the Bahá'í population has doubled and I don't feel so completely alone. It's too bad Boochie doesn't have a car so that we could make some calls – but we'll manage somehow.

The ad I put in the paper has not pulled any responses yet and, although I'm a little disappointed, I'm going to try another next week – a smaller one this time. I know how important it is to keep the name before the people and that responses take a long time. Perhaps this will be building an audience for Gerrit Vernhout when he comes in December.

I had a letter from the National Spiritual Assembly of Venezuela inviting me to the Bahá'í vacation school during the Christmas week, but it will not be possible for me to go because Vernhout will be here and I'm sure all my time will be needed here. Their letter also said that they had forwarded my suggestion, that a Dutch couple is needed here, to the National Spiritual Assembly of Holland. I still feel that is the answer for Bonaire. Even though I love this island and could consider living here for the rest of my life, I know that Tom and I would not be as effective for the Faith as those who are already fluent with the language. It would take us too long before we could serve the Faith as it must be served. We could, no doubt, add strength to a Dutch couple or a single pioneer but perhaps that would not be the way that we should be used. I know that Tom is just as content as I to go anywhere and be used in any way that promotes the best interest of the Faith.

This Bonaire experience has certainly convinced me that I am flexible and not too set in my ways to learn new things. Ponce de León set out to find the fountain of perpetual youth, it has been said. I offer that secret freely – it is simply to be continually excited and eager for new experiences; to try to enjoy pain and sorrow because of their enrichment values; to experience the impermanence of 'things'; to love deeply and to feel loved. I do not discount the value of good health and, possibly, the blessing of a good peasant heritage. It has occurred to me that the older I get, chronologically that is, the more I value my mother's peasant stock and devalue my father's patrician upbringing.

As I read this last, I find myself smiling. As if one could choose his forebears, as if one could deny his genes. Yet, I think that no one of us is so far removed from the earth and the agrarian society that we could not find our roots deeply embedded there if we looked. The values of our decaying and moribund society teach us to despise the dirt under our fingernails and to quicken to the sweet smell of 'success' as it preens itself in silks and perfumes. Everyone finds a line of 'nobility' or 'quality' in his bloodline. I am beginning to believe that the real 'nobility' lies in those honest virtues of patience, endurance, humility and courtesy, most of which I find here among the simple Antillians who have no pretensions to grandeur and no feeling of superiority.

Those of you who would learn about life and about living, get out of the sepulchers of your rooted lives. Throw off, without fear, the familiar garments of your accustomed ways and put on the filmy, easy robes of search. Climb out of the ruts that time and heritage have dug for you and step out into a new world. We call it 'pioneering'. I am just beginning to understand the meaning of 'going from an old self to a new'. There doesn't seem to be any way to change the 'old self' by staying in the same old place. The 'old place' is what helped to mold that 'old self' and, although change is possible any place, that change is accelerated and facilitated by a move to a new place and new values. If this 'hot-house plant' could benefit by being transplanted into a new world of change and uncertainty, other tender plants could also enjoy new and more rapid growth.

Sorry about that sermon. I told you that when I sit down to type, words come from my fingers through their own volition and not by conscious will of mine. I had not intended to speak of these things at all. I know I pour my heart out in these letters but some thoughts I probably should hang on to.

November 1
8:00 a.m.

My nephew did not come last night. I made two trips to the airport only to learn that he probably will not come until Thanksgiving time. His fractured rib would not permit him to do any scuba diving and that is one of the reasons he was coming. I'm a little disappointed. I had everything so ready but my disappointment is not nearly as keen as it would have once been. I know that I shall enjoy his visit whenever it happens. Now I shall look forward eagerly and with much excitement to my trip to Caracas in nine days. I count the days until Tom arrives and joyfully cross each one off the calendar as it passes.

November 6
1:30 p.m.

WELL, here I am sitting in the doctor's waiting room until 3:00 p.m. when office hours start again, having begun the long tiresome wait until my number is called. Numbers have not been distributed yet and, although I got here at 1:00 p.m. I was already the ninth arrival. Oh, well . . .

Number four 'whatever' has brought me here! A few days ago I began to notice a sore spot on my back and although I prayed it was only a continuation of what I had thought of as heat rash, I had a feeling it was a 'you know what'. I hope you do because I don't. They look like boils but the doctor has insisted, because of the deep hard core that almost always has to be cut out, that they are cysts. This 'thing' – by whatever name – is miserable and doesn't fill me with joy, in spite of my insistence that we must try to love pain because of its purifying value.

I treated 'number four' myself for as long as I could and got it to pop open but it is now inflamed and very painful. I am hoping that AFTER the doctor kills me, I'll get some relief. I am almost determined to have blood tests in Caracas when I finally get there. I say 'almost' because I'll be home in two and a half months and I'd rather hold out and do it in the States – for money reasons as well as reasons of convenience.

My trip to Caracas has followed the script faithfully so far. It has been another story of disappointment and delays. The plane ticket sent to me from the States had me leaving Bonaire on the 10th and staying in Caracas until the 17th. The chief purpose was to meet with the National Spiritual Assembly of Venezuela and discuss the ABC Islands teaching work. Since I have to go via Curaçao in any event, I wrote and suggested a Regional Teaching Committee meeting after the 17th – and possibly a local assembly deepening on the weekend of the 22nd and 23rd. This I wrote to Curaçao. The Curaçao Assembly had asked me to do it – and doing it this way would not involve any additional expense to the committee, the assembly or to me. I then wrote to my non-Bahá'í friend Tommy Antonczyk in Caracas and told her I'd be happy to be her house-guest, as she had suggested if I ever came to Caracas. Everything was set – Tommy was delighted, Curaçao made its plans and I mine. On November 4th, I got a telegram from the National Assembly of Venezuela asking me if I could come at a later date. They would not be meeting as an assembly until the 22nd and 23rd of November and hoped I could come at that time. With my departure only six days away I had to do some frantic juggling. As it now stands, I hope – this is dependent on confirmation from Curaçao and Tommy Antonczyk in Caracas – I'll leave Bonaire on the 15th (Saturday), do what I originally planned in Curaçao and leave for Caracas and my friend's hospitality on the 19th, making myself available to the National Assembly for the 22nd, 23rd, and 24th or, if necessary, on any day including the 20th and 21st. Tommy understands that the Faith has first call on my time. I must return on the 25th because I really expect my nephew Teddy to come on either the 26th or 27th to spend the Thanksgiving holidays with me.

Now that all that disappointing stuff is out of the way, I'm ready to share some good news. I know I wrote about 'Boochie' Statie last week but I didn't tell you that he has been with me almost every evening. I am teaching him English using a very simple Bahá'í illustrated course that was prepared by the Bahá'ís of Florida for teaching new believers. As simple as it is there are words like 'Manifestation', 'Messenger', 'Revelation', 'Guardian', 'Exemplar' etc. which I must translate into Papiamentu and then help Boochie pronounce in English and use. I feel that I am teaching on two levels: helping him learn a classic, beautiful English and deepening his knowledge of the Faith.

Now, 'Glad tidings No. 2' – I have found a seeker! We had a wonderfully deep fireside last night in spite of the fact that his languages are French and Arabic, neither of which I know. He speaks some Papiamentu and very little English. I cannot take credit for finding him – that belongs to Mr Mázgání. He had shown the Spanish film '*Paso a Paso*' at the Flamingo Beach Hotel and among those who attended was a young man from Lebanon, Michel, who evinced a strong interest. This was all Mr Mázgání could tell me – no last name, no address.

Now for the strange workings of intuition and guidance: next to the post office is a small grocery store which I pass every day. I had observed a serious young man, obviously not an Antillian, working there and I had a strong feeling that I would like to talk to him. But no graceful way became apparent. You know I'm not the lapel-grabbing 'have you heard the news, my friend' type. I waited. A few days ago I met, at the post office, a young woman with whom I have established a nodding, greeting acquaintanceship. She works at the grocery store. This was the first time I had been closely face to face with her. I asked her the name of the young man who works there and when she said, 'Michel', I asked if he was Lebanese. Yes, he was. I walked back to the store and found him. Usually he is in the back doing stock or out in the pick-up making deliveries or going for stock – but he was here and I introduced myself. Yes, he did remember Mr Mázgání – very happily. Yes, he did want to study more about the Faith. When could he come? That very night at 7:00 if that was all right with me. Was it? You bet! Well, he did come and we got along really well. The language problem IS a challenge but, as I remarked once before, if Bahá'u'lláh wants to get through, my ignorance won't stop Him. I gave Michel two pamphlets in Papiamentu and I hope I can find something in French or Arabic in Caracas. If not, I'll write to our Publishing Trust.

Michel has been here for two years. His uncle owns the grocery store where he works. When I asked him what he liked about Bonaire he said it was the tranquillity and quiet. He is a young man – more than 21, I would judge, but less than 30. He is rather good-looking in that swarthy, sultry, Arabic way that doesn't appeal to me as much as the clean brown look of the Antillians. He says he is an avid reader, hasn't made too many friends yet, loves to dance and frequents the local discotheque. I am sure he is subject to all the human weaknesses that flourish here but then I figure that's HIS problem. Mine is to expose him to the Teachings and let Bahá'u'lláh take it from there.

November 7
9:30 a.m.

I FEEL awful. In Papiamentu, 'Mi ta sintimi malu'. Dr Welvaart says that the blood tests I thought I should have are not necessary. He wants me to have a blood sugar test made tomorrow after lunch. He feels that the hypoglycemia may have reversed itself and it is possible that I am diabetic. He did a urine analysis that was negative – that's why he wants a blood test. In his opinion, that is what could have caused the series of disturbances I've had. Also he says that what I thought was heat rash was indeed – and still is – scabies. I never heard of that and he explained that it is a parasitic infection of which there has been an epidemic on three islands recently. My body was covered with it from scalp to toes and I'd had very little sleep for days – ever since Aruba, as a matter of fact. He gave me a prescription and assured me that, luckily, scabies is very easy to control. One or two applications of the ointment, plus bathing with an antiseptic soap, and it would be gone. If it were not for the pain of the 'thing' I'd feel great. At the moment, I feel miserable and I shall stop trying to type and go to bed. I stripped my bed and washed the sheets and all my towels and all my underwear and nightgowns; disinfecting them so that I won't be re-infecting myself. Doing that wash under the primitive conditions that exist here has taken every ounce of strength I had and my fingers stumble over these keys pathetically.

Same day
11:30 a.m.

DOCTOR told me to take aspirin for the pain and fever but I forgot to get any when I got the prescription filled and all I could get in the tiny 'tiendes' here is something the island people swear by and use almost exclusively. It is called Mejoral and it is potent. Last night I took two and felt drugged, but since I'm not used to aspirin either – rarely taking it – I thought that's the way aspirin would be, too. This morning I found out that Mejoral is used as a pain killer, is sold without prescription and that it works where nothing else will. It is supposed to be harmless and is considered here safer even than aspirin. Before I went to lie down I took another one and was able to forget the pain long enough to get a little sleep. It is as though all my energy is being used to fight the infection and all I want to do is sleep. I can't eat although I force-fed myself because of the blood test this afternoon.

Before I fell asleep it occurred to me that Bonaire was testing me to see if I deserved her. It seemed as if she wanted to see if I would cry 'uncle' and think of leaving. It is strange that never during any of the disappointments or the battles with the 'things' did I ever want to go home (that is, not for those reasons). I know that if it were my plan to spend the rest of my life here, all the nastiness would let up and I would have won the right to enjoy this beautiful island. So please, don't any of you waste time feeling sorry for me. Rejoice that I'm passing tests. OK?

Same day
1:30 p.m.

I'M waiting for the taxi to pick me up and take me to the hospital to have some blood drawn. Doctor wants me to see him on Sunday at 5:30 p.m. That blessed man works Sundays and holidays and is on call wherever he is needed. If I don't feel up to continuing this until next Monday, I'll be able to tell you what the blood sugar reveals. If it is true that I am diabetic, Tommy and I can go on the same diet and it will make cooking so simple. If I should be, don't start screaming for me to come home because I won't. I'm here for the 'duration' and I have no fear whatsoever, so don't any of you spoil this wonderful experience for me by sending negative thoughts this way. I never doubt that I am under His protection and you must not either. Sermon over.

November 9
7:15 a.m.

I HOPE this will make sense because I am forcing myself to type in order to keep from crawling back into bed. I don't want to see that bed until tonight. On Friday, I did go to have the blood drawn. Doie came for me and waited at the hospital to take me home. I had not been to *playa* at all on Friday. I was already too sick. Friday was a miserable night – no sleep at all. Nothing but waves and waves of pain. There was no position that I could be comfortable in and the Mejoral didn't help in the least. Saturday morning I sent Jacqueline to get Louie Martis for me. He has been coming in every day to see how I am. He says he does it to be sure I haven't died in the night. It seems he loves to read macabre stories and loves best the kind where someone was hale and hearty at dinner but was found stiff and cold the next morning. I once asked him what he would do if he did indeed find me dead. That threw him for a moment, then he spoke.

'Well, I would go to the Immigration and then to the post office.'

No use asking him why. I'm sure he would have told me and his answer was funny enough without an explanation.

I asked Louie to call the doctor for me and ask if I could come in Saturday because I knew I wouldn't have the strength to hold out against another sleepless night. Louie returned to tell me that the doctor was not available. Evidently his day off is Saturday. Another Dutch doctor in Rincón takes Dr Welvaart's emergency patients on Saturday. Rincón is several miles away; about a twenty-minute taxi ride. I was reluctant to make it but Louie has spoken highly of the doctor in Rincón and urged me to go. Miserable as I was, I wanted someone to tell me what to do. I was not able to make decisions for myself.

Well, dear old Louie did call the doctor and I'm grateful to him. The doctor was beautiful, physically as well as professionally. He confirmed my suspicion that the 'thing' had gone into secondary infection and was surprised that Dr Welvaart had not given me an antibiotic. I quickly covered for the doctor by explaining that on Thursday it wasn't so bad and that he wanted to see what the results of the blood tests were – and I really believe that's the truth. There was no reason, on Thursday, to believe that the condition would deteriorate so badly. Dr Scrivjer removed the bandage with the awful drawing salve, which alone was murder, and applied a wet dressing – over which he put a very clever, stretchy knit band that went completely around my waist and held the wet dressing – over which he had put one half of a thin rubber glove in place. He gave me enough antibiotic caps for three days but no pain pills.

When I pleaded with him – on the strength of my need for sleep – he said, 'You'll sleep tonight.' When I demurred he answered, 'If you don't sleep, you call me in the middle of the night and disturb my sleep. That will be my punishment.'

He was right. By the time Doie got me home, about 20 minutes, much of the pain had subsided and I did sleep much of the afternoon and much of the night. I feel much better this morning but weak and tired – and not too clear-headed. Now I wait for time to see Dr Welvaart and get the results of the blood test. I just know that will be OK.

November 10
2:30 p.m.

I DON'T know if I can write about yesterday without crying. The memory of pain is still so sharp and my shame at my behavior so great that I dissolve into tears just thinking about it.

I got to the doctor's office at 5:20. He was seeing

private patients by appointment only and, since I didn't expect to be long, I had Doie wait for me. I explained to Dr Welvaart that I had gone to Dr Scrivjer in Rincón on the day before because of the intense pain and I saw a strange look come over his face which, at the time, I could not interpret. He had me strip down to my waist and bend over his operating table, face down, rump up. He rather roughly took off the wet dressing with its plastic cover and, without saying a word, gathered up some instruments. He straddled me, a leg on each side of my legs and, still without a word, began to operate. That's the only word to use because that's what he did. I felt two sharp cuts, one up and one down. Then he began to 'express' by placing a thumb on each side of the incisions and squeezing. The pain was already mounting so that I could no longer hold myself and I began to scream. I'm sure I said things like, 'No, no. No more pain,' and 'Please, Doctor, don't hurt me anymore,' and 'Stop, please stop,' and many more foolish things like that. Of course he paid as little attention to me as if I had kept quiet. If he hadn't been straddling me and thereby holding me down, I'm sure I would have bolted and run for the door.

After the cutting and the squeezing began the digging and the tearing. I was aware that he was using several kinds of tools – all torturous. Altogether, I think I was under his hands about eight minutes and I don't ever want to live those eight minutes over again. I was hysterical when he finished, shaking and trembling all over and crying, of course. I told him that I hated him, that I wanted to hurt him – all those foolish, childish things – so unlike the lady of strength and character he had worked on the first time. I asked him why he hadn't given something to dull the pain beforehand and he said he didn't believe in them; he felt that strength must come from the mind. I asked him if he operated at the hospital without anaesthesia and he said he would if he could. So that's my nice kind doctor!

Well, when I got outside poor Doie was in a state. He had heard my screams and was in anguish for me. I was still sobbing when he got me home. To make things worse, Dr Welvaart didn't give me any pain pills so I anticipated a bad night. However, I was wrong. Whatever bad I can say about him he knew what he was doing – if only he would have done it more gently. Because I did have so much relief after my hysteria wore off, I was able to sleep most of the night. Today I am almost without any pain. I am to return to the doctor on Tuesday and, again, I dread it because I know there will be more probing and digging; but I know it will never again be as bad as it was. He had not received the results of the blood tests so I won't know that until tomorrow.

I try to tell myself that the reason for my bad behavior in the doctor's office was because I'd had three sleepless nights and four days of awful, constant pain; that I hadn't eaten much in two days and that I simply had not the strength to fight pain or anything else. I was so proud before to be able to say how strong I had been, what a brave soldier, and now to come out like a craven (that's the word, isn't it?) coward is rather deflating.

I know that all this must be finished before Saturday because I *will* leave for Curaçao – no matter what!

I hope to have a more cheerful tale next time. After all, what else can happen? And if that isn't tempting fate, I don't know what is . . .

November 11
6:45 p.m.

WELL, the waiting is over and it is just as I expected. I DO NOT HAVE DIABETES!!! I used to get so angry with my mother who was always able to diagnose her own illnesses before and better than any doctor. It annoyed me that she was so right so much of the time. Somehow it didn't seem right and, sharp as I was, I didn't hesitate to tell her what I thought. She would just laugh.

'Oh, some day you'll see. I'm not smarter than the doctor, I just know myself better.'

Well, I think I DO see because I'm afraid I'm just as much of a trial to my daughters in that respect as my mother was to me. Anyway, I could have told the doctor that I didn't have diabetes but since I didn't know, yet, what was causing the problem, I felt that I'd better shut up and offer my blood meekly.

Sometimes I think I outsmart myself by being so smart-alecky. Thinking that today's visit to the doctor was going to be so rough, I thought to prepare myself for the ordeal. In cleaning up my medicine chest I found one Darvon pill left from the first time the doctor worked on me and prescribed them. I figured that if I took it just before I went to his office there would be time for it to take effect before the nastiness on the table began. I was feeling pretty mellow when my number was called and could have taken much pain – not too badly – but the skunk decided not to do any digging today, just a change of dressing. Digging will continue on Thursday, thank you. So Thursday I go before the firing-squad without my blindfold. Neat little joke on me, huh?

More disappointments about the Curaçao–Caracas trip. This morning I had a telegram from Curaçao advising me that the 15th was 'inconvenient' and asking me to come on the 17th. This meant another trip to the ALM office and another change of ticket and it will also mean no local assembly deepening for Curaçao. The next two months, full as they will be, give me very little time for an extra trip to Curaçao.

Still haven't had a real confirmation from my nephew about when or if he is indeed coming this month. I'm toying with the thought of wiring him asking for a 'yes' or 'no'. I'm getting tired of hanging on the ropes.

I am anxious for the first crew of the tug boats to return. I had what I think is a beautiful idea. I'm going to ask Richard Swain, the captain of the *Ellen*, if he will let me bring Tom on board for a working cruise like the one I was on. I'm sure this will delight Tom and I'll bet Tom and Richard find lots to talk about – both being Mississippi River rats. It's true that Tom's Mississippi was a little north of New Orleans, but it's the same river, isn't it?

I didn't mention the dolphins. They play off the beach at the Hotel Bonaire almost every day, great big schools of them. They are such fun to watch and they seem to know they have an audience. I haven't been to the beach in almost two weeks because of this back and the rain, and I miss it very much. My beautiful brown skin is fading just a little and I'll have to hurry and brown fast if I'm going to take home that new Mimi I've been promising. Also, I haven't been able to do any yoga exercises for a week and I'm wondering how far that's going to set me back.

November 12
6:45 p.m.

Boochie was here last night and the evening took rather a different turn. I knew that Boochie had suffered a very serious head injury during a football game. He was one of the star athletes in the Caribbean when he was younger. He was usually selected for the All-Star games. His head injury almost cost him his life and left him with an impairment. When he gets overtired he gets 'foggy'. He's not dull by any means. He learns quickly and, when not fatigued, remembers well. He has a responsible job which he has held for ten years. When he was here last night I saw that he was dragging. I had seen him at the ALM office and he said he would see me that night. So, tired and dragging, there he was. I knew there was no point in trying to give him a lesson so I hit on the idea of letting him give me a lesson. I've been trying to learn some of the Bahá'í prayers in Papiamentu. I'd like to be able to memorize a couple of them.

I reasoned that I would ask Boochie to help me with the pronunciation of some of the more difficult words. He would read the prayers to me and then I would read them back for his approval. It worked beautifully. Although I had given him a prayer book in Papiamentu, he had not yet opened it – but as he read the prayers, he began to enjoy them and he would have read on and on if I had not begged him to give me a chance. As we read we discussed the words and why certain words were used – and it turned into a very satisfying and beautiful deepening. It also relaxed him and finally at 10:00 p.m. – after almost three hours – I had to ask him to leave. I think he could have gone on reading prayers all night. I also had the feeling that even though he, like most other Catholic boys, had served his time as an altar-boy, he was not given to prayers and/or praying. It was a good evening. I explained the use of the healing prayer, the 'Remover of Difficulties' and the noon-day prayer and his comment was interesting and astute.

'You know,' he said, 'the Seventh Day Adventists and the Jehovah's Witnesses also claim that if you read the Book of Psalms your troubles and sicknesses will go away. They also say that something "magic" happens. But I don't think they have the Word of God, Himself.'

I could have hugged him because I knew that whatever problems his earthiness and his body might get him into, his heart was where it should be. I know he will have to fight the same life-long battles with himself that we all must fight. Sometimes he will win and most times lose, like the rest of us, but I don't doubt his ability and his willingness to fight. The best help that I can offer him is that I believe God loves us as much for our efforts as for our victories. I'd better stop typing now before I preach another sermon – and God should spare you from that.

Same day
9:20 p.m.

I WAS sitting outside doing my evening 'thing' when my fingers began to itch to get to this machine. I had a letter to answer that was not letting me rest and my thoughts were getting heavy. I don't mean morbid, but deep – and I began to feel that they could become depressing if I didn't shut them off. Oh, for instance, as I was star-gazing I noticed something that I had remarked many, many times. The stars moved. I could see one peek up on the horizon and an hour later it would be high in the sky. I began to think about the sun. We say, 'The sun rises in the east and sets in the west'. Well, that's silly. It does no such thing. If I remember correctly, the sun is a fixed body. It doesn't move. *We* do. Yet such is the arrogance of man that he would be the center of the universe. He would have everything revolve around him, even that magnificent, life-giving FIXED body, the sun. It seems not possible for man to understand that this speck of dust we call the Earth is locked into a fixed pattern; that it has no will of its own; that it will, as long as it exists, be in thrall to the majesty of the sun and will forever revolve around that august body. No, the sun doesn't 'rise in the east' and all that. We might learn to say, 'We face the sun and are in light. We call light "day". We are turned away from the sun and enter the blue velvet dark we call "night".' But I guess man will play his little games and go on believing that he is the sum total of the universe and all was created for him;

that he revolves around nothing but that all things revolve around him. Do you see why I had to turn my mind off?

November 15
8:20 a.m.

ANOTHER little victory – and isn't that all that I asked for, little victories? Several weeks ago I accepted a lift from a man who, after bringing me home, came in and sat awhile talking to me. He, too, was anxious to speak informally and easily with an English speaker. His name is Jose Winklaar and he works as a waiter at the Hotel Bonaire. For all who serve the tourists here, ease with English results in larger tips and better jobs. I told him why I was on Bonaire and we talked about religion generally. He asked if he could come again and talk some more. Of course he could.

I didn't think I would ever see him again because that happened so often, but several days later – I think on a Saturday afternoon – he came again. I had asked him previously if he was married. He was. I learned that his wife works at the bakery where I buy that good brown bread. I suggested, at the first visit, that he give her my greetings. On this second visit, I asked him if he had told his wife of our talk and that he was intending to see me again. He said not only had he done that but that his wife wanted me to visit them in their home. That pleased me because I knew that our meetings would get off to a good beginning. I've been getting a little leary because to every man on Bonaire every woman means 'bed'. I never was in such a 'sex-oriented' society. They are very innocent about it.

After that second visit I didn't see anything more of Jose. Thursday I went to the bakery for another loaf of bread and spoke to his wife. She was very sweet and warm. I learned her name is Crisma. Yes, Jose had told her of our visits and she was very pleased. She hoped that soon I could come to visit them. My bread was still in the oven and, because I couldn't wait, she said she would deliver it to me. I paid for it and left. That evening Jose, alone, brought the bread. When I expressed disappointment that Crisma didn't come, he said that they were both getting ready to go someplace and that he couldn't stay – but he asked if I would like him to bring her to the house. I told him that nothing would make me happier.

'When?' he asked.

I replied, 'Why not tomorrow night?'

Fine, he would bring her. Although I had prepared myself for disappointment, I also prepared for the possibility that they would come. I bought a few 'goodies' and cleaned the house a little extra. After my dinner I sat out on the porch as usual with my tapes going and was enjoying myself again with the sights, the sounds and the smells that I'll carry with me the rest of my life.

At about 8:20 I had really given up on them but without any negative feelings at all. Just about that time a car pulled up and there they were with their nine-year-old son. They stayed until after 10:00. It was an easy, relaxed evening. Crisma has even less English than Jose and, believe it or not, I have more Papiamentu than they have English so most of the conversation was done in Papiamentu – with the help of my wonderful dictionary which I have now completed. I have done the English to

Papiamentu AND the Papiamentu to English! It was a great help to all of us this night.

I wonder if Jose or Crisma will ever understand by what gentle easy steps I led them to ask about the Faith. I knew they were Catholics but I didn't know how confirmed or unconfirmed they were – so I didn't want to do the 'missionary' job on them. I made casual, oblique references to the Faith – told a little of the history of the Catholic Faith, spoke of the good things the Fathers had done in the Antilles but also spoke of the work that still had to be done here and in the world.

Finally Jose asked, 'But what does it mean, Bahá'í?'

Crisma, whose Catholicism is stronger than his, I suspect, listened politely at first, and I had to be sure that no answer of mine would offend or hurt her. After awhile, she too began to ask questions and before very long we were enjoying a really good fireside.

It wasn't until Jose asked for something to read that I felt that some real progress had been made. This doesn't mean to say that I think he is about ready to become a Bahá'í. Will you have me flogged for heresy if I say I really don't care or think about that? Bahá'u'lláh makes Bahá'ís – we don't. We have been commissioned by our Faith to *tell* about it, to *offer* the information. That's all. I offered it. If Jose and/or Crisma or anyone else to whom I've given the Message responds that is the doing of their own hearts and the assistance of Bahá'u'lláh. But Jose is reading. I gave him things in both Papiamentu and Dutch.

This morning I tried to read one of the pamphlets in Papiamentu and was able to make out most of it. I hope the pamphlets in Dutch are better. We are so blessed in the States with the volume and the quality of our literature. There is so little available here. It is a wonder that anyone does catch a spark of that divine fire which comes through in English so beautifully – when *they* must read it in less inspired translations. How the Guardian must have loved us and how much he must have expected of us to have showered us with such magnificent works.

When leaving Crisma expressed the hope that I would soon be a guest in their house and I told her that I would be ready any time she sent Jose to get me. It probably won't be until I return from Caracas.

It has taken five months to break the ice here but I can see the water under the ice and I know fish are running there. It probably will take another five to six months before any results can be seen. Personally, I am a little wary of quick 'conversions' and if anyone imagines that by going into the travel teaching field they are going to gather stars for a crown (their crown) I think they are in for a disappointment. None of the people to whom I've been privileged to give the Message had first heard of the Faith from a Bahá'í but I'm sure their hearts had been prepared by the prayers and sacrifices of many of them. I don't know how to say this next so that it comes out as humbly as I feel. I pray for your deepest understanding. In spite of all the stories about the 'sacrifices' of the pioneers, I don't believe they are permitted to 'sacrifice'. Many pioneers have, indeed, given up a great deal to carry the Message of Bahá'u'lláh to places where life is difficult and presents many challenges. Their children suffer, their health deteriorates and their finances are depleted. But they are doing what they feel has to be done for the healing of the world and its people. I don't want to be put in any special category or made to feel special in any way because of this Bonaire experience. I haven't done anything. People don't treat us as 'special' because we breathe or move; well, serving the Faith in Bonaire has been just as natural and we deserve no accolades for doing what should be natural for all of us. What difference does it make where we serve the Faith – here or there? It disturbs me to see Bahá'ís brought to a platform and 'idolized' because they have done the most natural thing they can do.

November 31
3:45 p.m.

So many things have happened since I last wrote that I'm sure I'll not be able to recall with any sense of clarity all that I saw, felt or experienced. When I last wrote the Caracas trip and my nephew's visit were still very unsettled. Well, both happened. Both were very satisfactory and rewarding.

I left Bonaire on Monday, the 17th of November, for Curaçao. That night we had a Regional Teaching Committee meeting. It will be the last meeting I shall attend, in all probability. At the moment I see no possibility of being in Curaçao again, except between planes. It was a good meeting and I came away with a sense of having contributed to the work of the ABC Islands in a real and meaningful way.

The next night, by pre-arrangement, the English-speaking members of the Bahá'í community on Curaçao met at 6:30 at Dr Rabbani's house for a whirlwind run-through of the course for the deepening of groups. The purpose of that meeting was to brief them so that they would be able to use the course material for deepening with the entire community. They will use small sections of the material, which will have to be translated into Papiamentu, and plan deepenings for the whole year.

My sad experience on Aruba convinced me that the only way to reach many of the believers here is to give very small parts of any course but to give it in as much depth as would be required. The same course that might effectively be given in the States in five or six lessons would best be taught here in dozens of lessons. This is not because these people are stupid; they are not. But there has never been anything in their lives to prepare them even remotely to study in the way we are used to. They can certainly FEEL deeply but THINKING in terms of a new world order and new way of life requires careful and patient guidance.

I think it may help you to understand the learning preparedness of the Antillians when you know that, by law, they are required to go to school only to the third grade. Some progressive councilmen (as they are called here) are trying to get a law passed that will make it mandatory to go until the sixth grade. While there is very little illiteracy here, there has been very little 'in-depth' education. Everyone can read and write a little but it is the rare home that has a bookcase or that displays reading material other than the newspapers and the Bible.

While I was on Curaçao I had the two Rabbani sisters, both excellent doctors, look at my back. I'd had an appointment with Dr Welvaart on Bonaire for the Sunday night before I left but although I waited for more than a half hour, he didn't show up and I was so relieved that I almost cried. Doie, who had taken me there, laughed at my relief. I was actually terrified to see that doctor again. However, for whatever reason he didn't keep the appointment, I now felt completely justified in getting help elsewhere. The Rabbanis, both and instantly, said they felt the cause was a 'staph' infection and suggested I have a 'sensitivity test' made in Caracas and arrange to see a doctor there. Both of them told me that Americans were 'too clean'. When I protested that one couldn't be 'too clean', they pointed out that we were so antiseptic and sterile that our bodies weren't able to fight off bacteria that we encounter in other cultures; that we only build resistance by fighting and overcoming bacteria. All this registered in a vague way as I recalled some of the biology I had taken. I hated to be told that I was 'too clean' but I think I know what they meant.

When I got to Caracas the first person I spoke to – after I arrived at Tommy Antonczyk's apartment – was Carole Woodward, wife of the National Spiritual Assembly's secretary. I asked her if she knew a good doctor and told her my problem. She is a registered nurse in the States and has lived in Venezuela for several years. She told me that in Caracas one didn't need a doctor's prescription to go to a lab and have any kind of a test made. One simply went to the lab first and then to a doctor. She said she would come that very afternoon for me and take me to a good lab; that, when the tests were ready, she would make an appointment for me with a good doctor. Everything seemed so simple and so organized, just the way I like things. I should have known better!

There was no trouble at the lab. It was very much like a small hospital, immaculate and efficient. The technicians were well-trained and very professional. I was impressed. The first shock came with the bill – 160 Bolivas or US$40.00! All the money I had was 200 Bolivas which I brought with me. But I had already spent 40 Bs to get from the airport to Tommy's place. (No one met me at the plane because the secretary of the National Assembly was in the States when my wire giving estimated time of arrival reached there and no one had seen my wire – which, incidentally, had cost me 10 guilders, 50 cents – or about US$6.50). Then when Carole told me that the doctor would charge up to US$80.00 for the first (even though, only) visit, I really panicked. I wired Tom to put US$200.00 in my pioneer account AT ONCE because I knew I would have to write a bad check in Caracas and my only hope was that I knew it would take about a month for the check to clear my bank at home. So, even though I knew I was doing something awful, I did it with a relatively clear conscience. I prayed that Tom would have the money – but I know my beautiful, dependable husband and knew that if he didn't have it, he would get it. By the way, I've kept receipts for overseas calls (Curaçao, Bonaire, etc.) and cables to the States and I think they amount to more than US$50.00 – all because of mix-ups in scheduling, cancellations, etc.

Now it begins to get really hairy. When Carole asked the lab when the results of the tests would be ready, they told her, 'Not until Monday'. My return flight to Curaçao and Bonaire was scheduled for Monday morning. I knew I would have to see the doctor either Monday afternoon or Tuesday morning so I went to the

ALM office to change my reservation – only to be told that there was not ONE seat available on ANY flight to the islands for the next two weeks. If I didn't go on the Monday morning flight, I would have to stay in Caracas for two weeks. They wouldn't even put me on 'standby'. They said they already had more of a list than they liked. Carole and I consulted over it and came up with the only alternative plan. I would go to Curaçao on Monday. Carole would get the lab report on Monday and call it in to Nosrat Rabbani in Curaçao. Carole would interpret the report; Dr Rabbani would prescribe the antibiotic in the correct dosage. We called Nosrat on the overseas telephone to ask if she would do this. She would. So I left on Monday as scheduled and Nosrat met me at the plane and took me to her house to await the call from Carole. It came and Nosrat got the stuff for me at no charge – so I finally lucked out here, at any rate. No doctor's fee and no expensive bill for antibiotics. The wonderful end of the story is that although a fifth 'thing' began to show itself while I was in Caracas, the first day after taking the Penbritin that one disappeared and four days later all the infection from the fourth one had gone. Right now it is healing very well. It will leave a big scar, like the first one, but there is no sign of infection and no pain. I hope I can write 'finis' to the episode of the 'things'.

Caracas is a beautiful, modern city. It is situated in a large valley, almost a bowl, and is surrounded tightly by beautiful majestic mountains. The city is so large that it sprawls up the sides of the mountains on every side. Elegant and expensive homes surround the city. There is a lot of wealth concentrated here, but it is a city of slums as well. The poor people live in *barios* where tourists don't go. This tourist did, however, because some of the most beautiful Bahá'ís live there. Again, I was privileged to see, feel and experience Venezuela – at least a little piece of it.

Tommy lives right in the center of town in a 'Spanish' neighborhood. She is the only English-speaker there and has lived there for 26 years. She is very well known and liked although they consider her a little eccentric. She has no car so we walked all over Caracas.

I wish some Americans could see the marvelous buildings, the broad highways through town – and the traffic – unbelievable! Chicago or New York – at rush hour – couldn't be worse. I think it would knock out the sense of superiority that some North Americans feel in relation to other countries.

Tommy and I were taken to dinner by Don Newby, a pioneer here from the Middle West. He took us to the newly-completed development that is called 'a city within a city'. It even makes Rockefeller Center look small-town. We had a great dinner in a plush restaurant and spent almost two hours just gawking and looking. What that architect did with texture, planes and form, I have yet to see in the States.

I was introduced to Venezuelan food and am looking forward to preparing it for the friends when I return. The 'national' dish consists of black beans, rice and shredded meat cooked in a sauce. There are as many ways to cook the beans and meat as there are cooks but it always looks and tastes pretty much the same. I have learned to love *arepas* and have made them every morning for my nephew. These are made of pre-cooked white cornmeal and fried or baked. They are used the way we use bread. I have had sandwiches made with *arepas* and I have had them with butter, like toast.

Since Caracas is built on the mountainsides, walking in the *barios* is fun because some of the streets remind me of San Francisco: steep and hilly. Also there is, in some of the streets, the feel of Nazareth: narrow little passageways and steep down-grades. Streets are often made of cobblestone. Much color is used in the building material.

The one thing that bothered me in Caracas was the high noise level. I have never been in such a noisy city and – after the gentle, tender quiet of Bonaire – I was on edge most of the time. People speak so loudly, radios blare constantly and there is no restriction on street noise: automobile horns keep up a steady dissonance which deafens; motor bikes of every description run riot through the streets. I know why city people are so uptight; to be constantly battered by such awful noises is to be assaulted on every level of one's being. I think I should soon go mad there.

My meetings with the National Teaching Committee and the National Spiritual Assembly of Venezuela were most satisfactory. These are such overworked, dedicated people. A thousand pioneers wouldn't be enough to fill the posts that go begging for help. The National Spiritual Assembly and the National Teaching Committee work under such difficulties – my heart ached for them. Because of the nature of the situation under which they operate, organization as we understand it is almost impossible. Administrative *me* had to pull horns way back lest I offend or hurt these wonderful people who are working so hard to bring order to people who have never had it. Here, again, I learned that it is better NOT to do something than to hurt someone in the doing of it.

I attended the Feast of Qawl in the Ḥaẓírá in Caracas. I was able to contribute my little prayer in Papiamentu from memory and everyone was delighted. They asked me about the Faith on the ABC Islands and I was happy to tell about it. What I said was translated into Spanish and it was an interesting evening. I met a Bahá'í I had known in Chicago about 20 years ago. Her name is Addy Teske and she left to pioneer from Chicago that many years ago. She now serves on the National Spiritual Assembly of Venezuela and she is now Mrs Alford. Her husband is a Bahá'í. I had dinner at their little house in one of the *barios*. Although their means are very modest they are serving the Faith wonderfully.

I returned to Bonaire on Monday night and wrote a long letter to the National Assembly of the United States to try to answer some of their questions about living here. Maybe it will be useful to a prospective pioneer.

Dearly-beloved friends,

At your request I am sending you the information about living conditions on Bonaire, with one or two recommendations.

Some food prices, in guilders first, then in American dollars:

Canned Tuna Fish, solid, 7 oz	2.20	1.22
Canned Pineapple, medium size	1.49	.90
Vinegar, 12 oz	1.73	.98
Corn Oil, 48 oz	5.65	3.14
Jello, 3 oz	.34	.25
Ground Beef, lean, 1 lb	3.29	1.82
3 Green Peppers	1.60	.96

6 oz Minute Maid Orange Juice	1.06	.64
1 Lemon (when available)	.29	.16
3 lbs Rice (white)	3.49	1.84
1 lb Butter	1.89	1.06
Lettuce (when available)	2.00	1.15
Stretch and Seal Plastic Wrap (small)	1.39	.83
Eggs, 1 dozen	2.50	1.50

Sugar and Coffee are also pretty high. Bread is very cheap. There is an excellent bakery that sells good brown bread for .65 Antilles or about 39 American cents. I think the prices listed above, although very incomplete, are indicative of the general trend in food prices. Most vegetables are hard to get. Cucumbers and green peppers seem to be readily available but lettuce and tomatoes are not always on the market. Avocados sell for 1 guilder or about 60 cents and are often seen in the markets.

If one's tastes and one's appetite are not too large it is possible to manage. Housing is expensive. Once the lease on this house is up next year I am sure the price will go up. It would easily rent for 150 guilders or US$90, unfurnished. Utilities are high and one pays for water. My electric bill for September was about US$15 and I use it very sparingly. As I review the above prices I see that they really are not bad. I am certain that if someone had an income of US$300 a month he could live here not too badly. Autos are expensive but taxis are reasonable. For 60 cents one can ride a taxi-bus from town to home. Mostly I walk, though!

The climate is ideal for one who can take damp heat. It never gets terribly hot but the dampness makes for discomfort. Mosquitoes and other flying pests are not too troublesome on Bonaire. They were much worse on Curaçao and Aruba. The water is pure and clean. Since none of the houses we could afford are air-conditioned, one or two good electric fans are really necessary. Cooking is done by bottled gas which is not expensive. I realize that I am rambling; I am trying to think of all the small things that might be helpful and I haven't organized my thinking beforehand. I apologize.

I would strongly recommend that any pioneer coming to these islands have a complete physical check-up before coming and go on a Brewer's yeast and yogurt diet for at least two months before coming and be prepared for anything. I have been told that Americans are 'too antiseptic and sterile' which leaves them prey to bacteria unfamiliar to their systems. I would also suggest that a good supply of vitamins be brought in and a good first-aid kit with a good sunburn lotion.

Writing-paper and paperback books are very expensive. For a pad of 50 sheets of typewriter paper (this) that costs 85 cents in the States, I paid US$1.25; for a paperback book that costs 90 cents in the States, I paid US$2.00.

Anyone coming to any pioneer post would be wise to do a heavy campaign among his or her friends and get them committed to writing often. No one who has not experienced it can imagine the awful lonesomeness and, sometimes, hopelessness that overtakes you when you are separated from the friends. All the praying in the world doesn't take that away the way a letter from home will. Money gifts from friends who love you and who offer it from the heart are wonderful, but the sacrifice of time and thought that goes into the writing of a letter really show the degree of love in a much more meaningful way.

I would not have missed this experience for all the money in the world or any title the Faith could bestow. I shall always remember Bonaire and love it dearly, for it was here that I really found out who and what Marion West is. Here I learned to balance the warring elements that exist in all of us. When I return to the States I shall be the best advocate for pioneering there is. But I shall also counsel caution and a proper evaluation of one's real nature. How much do you need the 'world'? How many internal resources have you? How adaptable do you think you can be? These are the questions that should be answered.

You will be happy to learn, as I was, that Rhoda Vaughn is planning to return to Bonaire on or about the 10th of January.

I hope, dear friends, that I have answered the questions you wanted information on. As soon as I return to the States I will send you a copy of the English–Papiamentu, Papiamentu–English dictionary that I have compiled. I have only one copy and it would cost a fortune to do it here. I shall be home the end of January and by the middle of February your copy will arrive, as will one for Rhoda. Please understand that it is not a complete vocabulary list. It consists only of words I found in Giolo's Papiamentu Textbook. It will be very helpful, however, to anyone who really wants to learn Papiamentu – which is a very simple language and can be learned in just a few months. I should like to add that Antillians take a very dim view of anyone who comes to live here (that is, not a tourist) who will not learn the language. While they are the nicest, most gentle of people (in Bonaire at least) they have very harsh things to say about the Trans World Radio people and the Dutch who come here to work in the oil industry and who, even after 20 years on the island, don't try to speak Papiamentu. I think that my blundering but sincere efforts to learn has done much to endear me, and the Faith, to the Bonairians.

If you need or want any other information, let me know and I'll get it to you at once.

With deepest love and gratitude for your kindness,

Marion West

On the Wednesday morning after my return from Venezuela I had a cable from my nephew telling me that he would arrive THAT night. He did and we have had the best time I've had on the island.

I rented a car for him at his request. When he arrived he said that he had come with lots of money and that he wanted to spend it all on me. He did! We ate in the best restaurants on the island and I finally had *rijstaffel* and *nasi-goreng*, fabulous rice dishes from Dutch Indonesia. We drove all over the island; every bay and every road was examined. He is a great adventurer and we explored and tried everything. On one of our trips we had as a guide the councilman that I had met before I left for Caracas. He showed us parts of the island that we would never have seen and explained everything. He's going to be a good friend of the Faith. Teddy left on the morning plane today and already I miss him. He was a wonderful surprise. I hadn't seen him in years and didn't know what to expect. He's a really great guy and I had a wonderful visit with him.

Now I am awaiting news about whether or not I'll be going to the Falkland Islands. If I go, I'll be hard-pressed to get everything ready for Mr Vernhout – but I do so want to go. So as usual, I'm hanging fire – just waiting. I'll let you know.

December 6
3:50 p.m.

THIS is going to be a thoroughly disjointed account. There is nothing special to report and nothing noteworthy has happened so I will pick up some loose threads and, for the rest, see what thoughts come off the top of my head.

First of all, and probably important, is the news that my trip to the Falkland Islands has been cancelled. While I was in Caracas I had a cable from the International Goals Committee in the USA saying they were having difficulties in booking flights to the islands and asking if I could possibly go a week later or in January after leaving Bonaire. My cabled reply was that I could go the week later *if* they could get me home (to Bonaire) by the 23rd so that I could be here when Mr Vernhout arrives. I also said that I could not possibly go in January, that Tom and I were returning to the States because of his job. Well, again I began that uncertain wait for confirmation. Was I going and when, or was I not going? Finally, as the deadline time approached with no confirmation, I cabled asking for some word. The reply said simply that it was not possible to schedule flights within the time slot and that the trip would be cancelled for the present. I am both relieved and disappointed. I'm relieved because now I will have ample time to make proper arrangements for Gerrit's visit and assure some audience for him; disappointed because the Falkland Islands represent the end of the world to me and most of my Bahá'í life they have been the 'unattainable'.

I remember that for many years we tried to get settlers on that remote place. I know how much the Guardian wanted those islands settled. Never, in my wildest dreams, did I see myself there. I know how remote and desolate they are and I longed to bring the love of the Faith and the warmth I felt for those devoted pioneers to them. I didn't kid myself into thinking I had any special knowledge to bring them. I knew John Leonard was there and I'm sure he knows more in one minute than I'll ever know about teaching the Faith – but I did know that my heart was full of love that I longed to share with them. Now I longed to bring the warmth and peace and gentleness of Bonaire to them. I recall how, when dear, dear Hand of the Cause Mr Furútan met Tom and me at Geyserville shortly after our return from pilgrimage, he told us we still had 'the Haifa smell' – and I am sure that now I have a Bonaire smell and I want so much to spread it over all Bahá'ís. So you can see the quality of my ambivalence. But I am relieved that there is no longer uncertainty and I can relax.

Today it has rained constantly. The rain began last night about 9:00 and has not let up for more than a few minutes at a time. I am told that this is most unusual. Actually, we have had rain every day for the past four days. It has been cool enough at night so that a light covering is needed in bed. Imagine, winter on Bonaire – unbelievable!

Louie Martis came by, in the rain, to see if I was all right. He stayed awhile and talked. He told me that when he was a boy there used to be much rainfall on the island and that at that time the island was very different. There were many crops grown and many fruits. He said watermelons were a bountiful crop and brought much revenue to the island. He also said they had large herds of cows, goats and sheep and that there were many horses on Bonaire. Today, there are no horses or cows, just a few sheep and lots of goats but not nearly as many as formerly. He said his father, alone, had owned 2500 goats. Hard to imagine. It seems that after the First World War the rains stopped and gradually the island became the desert it is now. That reminds me of the joke Tom and I like so much. Two cavemen are sitting in front of their cave watching an electric storm. One says to the other, 'We never had storms like this until they began to use bows and arrows.' Well, evidently Louie blames the weather – or lack of it – on the war! Dear Louie has offered to clean my walls and ceiling before Tom comes. Cobwebs gather in all the corners and it is so difficult for me to get at them. My one broom won't get into the corners.

Another wonderful and mysterious thing happened today. I'm not prepared to evaluate these events, they just happen. I was busy at my typewriter when I saw a man come around to the back of the house. I went to see who he was and what he wanted. He said he had come to read the electric meter and I greeted him.

'How is Bahá'í going?' he asked.

I almost fell over but recovered long enough to ask him if he knew of the Faith. It develops that he is the son of the man who called Curaçao for information about the Faith in response to a TV program – and whom I had been trying to reach ever since I got to the island. I had spoken to the father on the phone and had told him that I would come to see him. At that time he had said that he would come to see me. He never showed up and was one of the disappointments I wrote about. I asked Jan, the son, in and gave him some literature in Dutch. He said the reason his father hadn't come was that he got sick and then other things intervened but he was sure he would come now. I guess if I stayed here another seven months I'd eventually see all those whose names I got when I first came here. Well, Rhoda can pick up the trail from here. By the way, Boochie knows all those I had hoped to reach and he has promised to have them at the public meeting when Gerrit Vernhout speaks.

This brings me to the next bit. It has been next to impossible to find a place for that meeting. The Flamingo Beach Club, where Mr Mázgání had his meeting, is no longer available and there is no public library large enough – it is just a small room and not suitable. The only place I could find was a dancing school that would not be used for classes during the holidays but that was taken for the evening that we would want it. We can have the place either Saturday or Sunday afternoon. I got Boochie to check this out for me and was told that the charge would normally be 150 guilders or US$90.00 but, because Boochie was a friend of the man in charge, we could have it for 50 guilders or US$30.00. I think I can manage that plus a small ad in one of the papers. So plans for Vernhout are shaping up. I'm going to do a private mail invitation, too, to several people.

Another bit of encouragement. Remember Mr Sweebie, the Jamaican who didn't come to dinner? I haven't seen him since that time and I'm sure it has been shame that has kept him away – even though I did send him messages through Dee Reed. A few days ago Mr Reed told me that Sweebie had said that he wanted some Bahá'í books to take back to Jamaica with him. The project at the terminal is completed and all the men are leaving pretty soon. The Reed family is going on the 17th of December; Sweebie will be among the last to go in February. I told Mr Reed that Sweebie knew where I lived and that I would be happy to give him Bahá'í books if he came for them. At least some interest is there, so I'm pleased.

The expensive ad I put in the paper has not brought specific results but I know it has been seen because every once in a while, upon learning that I am a Bahá'í, some one will say, 'Oh, are you the one who put that ad in the paper?' I guess we have no way to measure the results of anything we do for the Faith.

My dictionary is finally complete and it was a bigger job than I thought it would be. Not satisfied with doing an English to Papiamentu listing, I decided to do one from Papiamentu to English. It is very incomplete. I doubt if there are 2000 words in either list. But that is more than has ever been done before. I spoke to the director of the Tourist Information Center, a government agency, about my idea of putting a copy in every hotel room. He was very impressed. I even showed him how it could be made to pay for itself. I'm sure that the businesses on Bonaire would pay for space for advertising in such a booklet. He was sure they would too.

Before I left his office he told me that on December 14th there was going to be a unique program on the island. It would be in the nature of a contest where writers from the three islands would offer poetry, prose, stories, etc., all in Papiamentu in an effort to develop a literature in the language. There is none at present. The man responsible for the program and the inspiration for the whole event has done a Papiamentu to Dutch dictionary and would be the ideal one to help me polish mine. Nicky Tromp, the tourist bureau man, is going to bring this man to my house to meet me. I will offer my list to them as a gift of love to Bonaire and hope it will be used.

Same day
6:30 p.m.

I'VE just finished my dinner and, although it has stopped raining, it is overcast and dull outdoors. It is not pleasant enough to sit out there so I've decided to finish this tonight. I'll probably be sorry tomorrow when I'm faced with a Sunday with nothing to do. I don't even have a book left that I haven't read at least once. Oh well, tomorrow will just have to take care of itself.

I'm feeling a little sad, realizing that next month I'll be home and there won't be any more *Letters from Bonaire*. If you have enjoyed receiving them, your joy cannot compare with my joy in writing them. I used to chide

Tom about the verbosity of his letters; I would tell him that anything worth saying should be said in few words. He is too generous and kind to remind me of those words but I'm sure it must have occurred to him that my letters are anything but 'terse'. I find that I too am saying so little in so many words!

I have been wanting to share with you some of the exotic names of the trees on Bonaire. When I was a little girl the sounds of the strange, far-away places would be enough to set me off running away from home. I love the wonderful sounds of these trees that I had read about but never thought to see. How about:

Bougainvillaea	Hibiscus
Jacaranda	Kapok
Flamboyant	Divi-divi
Cup of Gold	Tamarind

and how about aloe and prickly pear cactus or juffrouw? How about dozens of fern trees whose names I haven't learned? I suppose those of you who live or have lived in southern states will find this 'old hat' but this city girl from the north finds it deliciously exotic.

Did you know that the bark of the jacaranda was used by the Indians to heal skin diseases and that there is a large cactus tree that bears a sweet fruit like a fig? Or that the aloe plant has great cosmetic and medicinal value? Would you believe that from the sticky, prickly cactus, called here cadushi, they extract a marvelous spice, highly prized? Teddy, my nephew, was lucky enough to get some of it from my friend, Siegfried Pourier, one of the councilmen on Bonaire. When Siegfried heard Teddy say he wished he knew how to get some of it (it is not sold commercially) Siegfried got a friend to make some for Ted. And I found out that the stuff we call kapok and use for stuffing mattresses and so on actually comes from a tree. The tree bears a fruit and the fruit has pods. When the pods are dry, they pop open and inside is a cotton-like stuff that is kapok. I'm getting an education that no school can provide – at least none I ever went to.

It has started to rain again. It will soon be 24 hours of continuous rain. Do you remember that I once said that there is an abundance of everything here? When this place gives – it gives! I will be very happy to see the sun again.

I have made all flight reservations for our trip home and this time I didn't even ask if we were flying in the little plane or the big one. Since the time I said I wouldn't fly in the little plane I have three times and I'm beginning to like it. It isn't really as scary as I thought it was that first time. See, when the unfamiliar becomes the familiar, even fear goes.

December 8
3:40 p.m.

WELL, I weathered Sunday all right. It rained without let-up all day and only the good fortune of finding a copy of *QB VII* by Leon Uris tucked away in some cartons made the day endurable. I had read *QB VII* before but it is a very re-readable book and it held my attention all day and evening until I finished it. Occasionally, when my eyes would get blurry, I'd stop and type a letter. I've finally caught up on all my correspondence. There is not a single unanswered letter left and I'm pleased about that, except if I don't get some more letters, I may find myself at loose ends again with nothing to do.

It poured all night but at about 8:30 this morning the clouds parted and my dear, sweet friend, Mr Sun, came out smiling and blessing the island. I hurried to *playa* while it was still sunny. I got to the post office (nothing there), the drug store and the supermarket just before the rain started again. I was lucky to get a taxi before the deluge. It started to pour and is still coming down in sheets. This makes seven continuous days of rain, and although it is getting a little wearing, I am still caught up in the splendor of it. I've run out of 'projects' however and, unless my sometimes fertile brain becomes infertile, I'll think up something to do should this prove to be a '40-day rain'.

I must tell you something that finally happened between Mrs Reed and me. I was about to say 'something that amused me' but I got scolded once for using that expression about something that someone DIDN'T think was amusing – so I'm a little wary about using it! It DID amuse me, though. There, I've said it!

I hadn't seen the Reeds for a long time. They had gone to Curaçao to shop and I had gone to Caracas. One day, on a Saturday when it wasn't beach weather, I had Doie drive me over there and leave me for a couple of hours to visit. Mr Reed was home too. We had a very pleasant visit for awhile.

Then Inez said, 'We missed you so much. I told my husband that I love you so much I pray for your soul every day.'

'That's wonderful, Inez,' I replied, 'but why are you so concerned about my soul?'

'Well, if I could only make a Christian out of you and get you away from that silly thing you're in.'

I asked her what she knew about my Faith, if she had read any of the things I had left with her. She answered that she had and they were nonsense. I asked her if I had ever indicated to her that her Faith was nonsense. I asked her if I had ever made any attempt to destroy or belittle her very strong faith. She allowed that I hadn't and she said she wanted me to argue my Faith with her and she would listen.

I said, 'I will never *argue* my Faith with you, Inez, because I know that while I am speaking you will not be listening. Your mind will be busy framing arguments without even hearing what I am saying.'

Dee, her husband, clapped his hands at this point and said, 'Oh MIMI, do you *know* her! She won't listen because she doesn't want to hear anything about your Faith!'

Inez laughed and said, 'If you haven't been baptized by the blood of the Lord, there is no salvation for you and I worry about you.'

Now, I know that Inez is a good and sincere woman. Jesus is her way of life, she leans on Him, she clings to Him, she belongs to Him – and she does love me. There isn't a mean or vicious thought in her.

I finally said, 'Inez, you belong to Jesus just as I belong to Bahá'u'lláh. I don't pray for your soul – I leave that to you. Please leave the condition of my soul to me and we will remain friends forever.'

To prove what a fine person she is, none of this left any scars and we have been together several times since then. Her faith in Jesus is purely emotional but it is strong. She has no knowledge of the history of religion or how the Bible came to be. She believes that every word it contains is the Word of God. I suppose I could try to shake her faith with knowledge – if I could get her to open her ears and mind – but I can't get myself to do that. She is as good as she can be and she has heard about Bahá'u'lláh. I prefer to let it rest there – besides which I'm sure her prayers for my soul can't do anything but good.

December 14
5:50 p.m.

FINALLY, a Sunday I didn't resent! I spent all day at the beach. Doie got me there at 10:00 a.m. and was to pick me up at 2:00 but I was enjoying it so much that when he came I asked him to come back for me at 4:00. I've been at home long enough to feed the cats, do my exercises, shower and eat. But it has been a lovely day – the first one I've had at the beach for weeks. In just this one day I've regained most of my tan.

It was a wonderful day for many reasons. Raphael's father and his two sisters were at the beach when I got there. It had been a long time since I had seen them. Poppi, the older sister (about 17) and I have a nice thing going; we like each other. It was Poppi who took me to the Bonaire Hotel beach the very first time. Mr Statie speaks no English and seems a little shy with me but since Poppi wouldn't let me speak English – she insisted that I speak Papiamentu – Mr Statie soon warmed up. It was fun being with them and speaking to them entirely in Papiamentu.

I also met two charming little people this day, Jessica and Roy – a brother and sister who were with the Staties, although the children had not come with them, nor did they leave with them when the Statie's left the beach at about 12:00. The children stayed with me and I found them completely enchanting. Again, we spoke nothing but Papiamentu and I found myself being taught by a little girl. The children live in Noord Salina, which is north of Antriol, and they walk to the beach every Sunday. It's quite a hike but they don't think anything of it. Because I was going to stay so long, I had lunch at the Beach Hut and invited the two little children to eat with me. All three of us are looking forward to next Sunday. It has to be a wonderful day when you meet three old friends again and meet two delightful new ones.

Last night I went to a Christmas concert given by the Trans World Radio people. It was a free concert but you had to have a ticket to get in. I had asked Doie to come for me but he told me that his wife was going with some friends and he would ask her if there would be room for me. There was. I'm still trying to sort out my feelings about the concert. Musically and theatrically it was beautiful. It was a most professional job. The staging was exciting, the voices really good amateur voices, the music excellent, there was enough novelty so that it wasn't boring – and I know you're all waiting for the 'but'.

Well, there was a 'but' and I found myself wanting to cry during the performance. If anyone had noticed they would have imagined that I was getting sentimental about the Christ-child theme. I'm glad mental telepathy hasn't been perfected – because I'd probably have run out of there if they could have guessed what made me want to cry. As I have said, everything was beautiful. The first half of the program thrilled and pleased me. They used only the very best Christmas music – no 'Jingle Bells' or 'Santa Claus is Coming to Town'. They used a great deal of Handel and some beautiful old German, Portuguese and French carols that I had never heard before. There were several selections for bells, a flute solo and a masterful trumpet solo. So my heart rejoiced at the good music and, of course the beautiful theme awakened the love I have felt for Jesus since I was a child. But the last part, which was a Christmas cantata, was the thing that 'done me in'.

The narrator began by saying that while there had been fir and pine trees for centuries and holly berries and mistletoe, nobody knew what to do with them until the year 1 AD when Christ was born. That was the first time I wanted to get up and say, 'Hey, wait a minute. You'd better brush up on your ancient history and religious rituals.' He said that not until 1 AD did it occur to anyone to hang lights and garlands on a tree and it was not until then that anyone thought of exchanging gifts. It all happened because the three wise men brought gifts to the baby Jesus. And that the reason Jesus was born was because God felt sorry for man, who didn't know about God, and He decided to come down from His glorious realm and live like a mortal among men; that He decided not to come down in His robes of purple and gold but to come down like a child born of woman. The more he talked, the more I felt I was listening to a course in mythology. Then he continued by saying that when Jesus came He brought the peace mankind had been looking for – and I wanted to scream at the poor man and ask what fairy tale he had found THAT in – what peace was he talking about! All of these outright lies he was handing out were tucked in between some very good singing and instrumental music. Just when I'd relax and feel that the music was worth the price of having to listen to his foolishness, he'd begin again. Really I wanted to cry because all the people in the audience – and there must have been two hundred – seemed to accept all that without question. How blind is blind? Where are the independent thinkers? The script, which the narrator read beautifully, had so many inconsistencies and inaccuracies that I could type for hours pointing them out. But I learned one very important thing last night. The love songs that are sung to and about Jesus, the tenderness they evoke, the pride generated by knowing and loving Him – all these are what have kept good and sincere people in the churches. One must walk away from two hours of praising and glorifying Him and hearing again the tender-sweet story of His birth with renewed conviction about one's belief in Christ. Remember this has been going on for many generations and it elicits an almost Pavlovian response. Listen to the Christmas music; hear again the Story and, once again, you're saved! I wonder how many generations of hearing the story of the sufferings of Bahá'u'lláh it will take before we respond so profoundly? Or is this a kind of heresy?

December 19
6:10 p.m.

THESE letters from Bonaire seem to be drawing to a

close. This morning ended the episode of the Reed family. I saw them off on the plane to Curaçao where they will get the plane to Kingston, Jamaica. Their going was a comedy in itself. They had been scheduled to leave on the 10:05 plane Wednesday morning and I had Doie take me to the airport so that I could see them off. That's rather a ritual here; I suspect it's another way the island people create excitement for themselves. 'Going to the airport' becomes something of a social event: friends meet, the bar is well patronized, children play, bets are placed about the arrival time of the plane (which rarely comes at the scheduled time). There is much hugging and kissing and lots of laughter.

However, Wednesday morning was not quite like that. The first three planes out in the mornings used to be the 19-passenger 'Otters' but they had to be shipped to Saba (another island in the Lesser Antilles group) for reasons that are not really relevant. So Bonaire was being serviced by the tiny nine-passenger Beechcraft. The Reed family, with lots of luggage, were the only passengers booked on the 10:05 flight. We watched the flight that was scheduled to leave at 9:10 leave at 10:20 because of the extremely heavy rain storm and gusty winds. It was to have gone to Curaçao with its few passengers (a matter of 20 minutes), turn around and come back for the Reeds. I waited with the family until about 11:00 and, expecting the plane to return any minute, said my farewells to them and left. Later that afternoon Doie stopped by the house and told me that the plane never did come back; that because of the violence of the storm in Curaçao, no more planes would come that day. The airport was closed and the four Reeds were deposited, at the expense of ALM at the Hotel

Bonaire. Doie thought they would leave the next day but I was sure they wouldn't because there are only three planes out of Curaçao for Jamaica in the week – one on Monday, one on Wednesday and one on Friday. So I knew my friends would be at the hotel all day Thursday and I arranged with Doie to pick me up in the morning and take me to the hotel. I spent the whole day there, had lunch at the hotel with them and visited with them and kept them from feeling the disappointment too much. We really had a good time.

This morning they did leave on the big jet at 11:20 and I'm sure they were happy to get home. They have been here for almost one year. If ever I should get to Jamaica I know I would receive a warm and loving welcome from the Reeds.

The rains have been excessive; only one day of sunshine this week and I spent most of that day at the beach. This afternoon, late, the sky cleared and there is promise of good weather tomorrow.

I'm terribly disappointed at not getting any clear confirmation about the arrival of Gerrit Vernhout. While I have made his hotel reservations (which can be cancelled if necessary), I haven't been able to get a place for a public meeting nor have I been able to do any publicity for him. I'm beginning to feel that the things that have characterized my stay on Bonaire have been the waiting for developments and the uncertainty – and, of course, the disappointments. The hall and the publicity depend on my knowing exactly when he will be here and for how long. This is another thing we'll have to 'play by ear'.

December 30
10:00 a.m.

It's been a long time but finally I am alone and able to gather my thoughts. Gert (short for Gerrit and pronounced Ghett – with a little gargle on the 'gh') did arrive late on the night of December 23rd. I'd had no word at all about his arrival until 3:00 on the morning of Tuesday the 23rd when Raphael woke me to deliver a strange message. The Bahá'ís on Curaçao know that Raphael works at the Flamingo Beach Hotel so they called him there and asked him to get a message to me. I was supposed to call Curaçao *before* 8:00 that morning. Raphael worked until 3:00 a.m. so that was the soonest he could give me the message.

Well, there was no way for me to call before, or even at, 8:00 but I knew that there was a plane due at 8:00 and I reasoned that's what they wanted to tell me – that Gert would be on that plane. So I went to Doie's house a little after 7:00 and he took me to the airport. Of course, you've already figured out that Gert was NOT ON THAT plane!

I went back into town and called Curaçao. Gert answered the phone and explained that he was coming in on the 9:30 p.m. flight! They asked me to call early – not realizing that it would be a problem – because he had some calls to make early in the morning. When I told Doie he was coming in on the 9:30, Doie said there *was* no 9:30 plane. Oh, it was such a mix-up!

Expecting Gert in by afternoon I had bought two tickets for a Christmas Community Concert – another concert! I arranged that Doie would take me to the concert hall, go to the airport and get Gert, give him his ticket and bring him to the concert, after which Doie would call for us and take Gert to the hotel. The concert was over at 10:00. No Doie, no Gert. I begged a ride to the airport and found it closed tight. The couple who gave me the lift took me to Doie's where I learned that Doie had met the 9:00 p.m. flight (which was the scheduled night flight) and Gert was not on it and no one mentioned anything about an extra plane (which, in fact, is what happened).

I prevailed on the generosity of the couple and asked them to take me to the Hotel Rocheline on the chance that Gert might be there. He was. When I had reserved the room for him they showed me a fairly decent room with air conditioning. But the room they actually gave him was horrible and the air conditioning didn't work. However, relieved that he was on Bonaire, I went home.

Early the next morning I walked to the hotel to find that Gert had checked out the night before – around midnight. I was thrown. I didn't know what to do or where to look – but, as I was walking away from the hotel, I was hailed by Gert from an auto. Unable to sleep because of the heat and the stuffiness, he had gone out on the street and hailed the first friendly face he saw and asked about another hotel. The young man took him first to the Flamingo Beach, which was full, and then to Hotel Bonaire where Gert was able to get a room for only that night for US$42.00 a night! When I met him in the street, he was really down. I simply had no choice but to do what I had offered to do originally – have him stay with me. He slept in the bed I rented for my nephew and for Tom and I'm so happy he was with me. Then, on the morning after that first day, Wednesday, a brand new Bahá'í from Curaçao joined us. He slept on the floor the first night and Doie's wife took pity on him and let us borrow a canvas cot. So I had two beautiful Bahá'ís staying me and it was heavenly.

Manuel Maduro is a young man of 31. He and his father have a clothing store on Curaçao. He became a Bahá'í while Gert was on Curaçao before he came here to Bonaire. He is on fire with the Faith and is already a marvelous teacher. He had first been a Roman Catholic, then a Seventh Day Adventist. He knows scripture like I know the a,b,c's, is very articulate and well educated, is good to look at and completely dedicated. Gert and I had four never-to-be-forgotten days of deepening him. I never had the pleasure of teaching such a sponge!

Once again I had the pleasure of cooking for men – and could those two eat! We were a happy, united little family for those few days. While I cooked, they studied; when I washed dishes, Gert dried and Manuel swept the floors. We prayed together in the morning, in the afternoon, in the evenings; and sometimes we were so exhilarated we couldn't sleep, so we got up in the night for prayers. We achieved such closeness we were like one body. It was heavenly.

None of the plans I had made in my mind for Gert's visit materialized; nothing went according to plan, but things worked out so beautifully. Together, we were able to give the Message to dozens of people who listened. My friends Jose and Crisma came to the house twice for firesides and once they invited us to their house where we had an exciting time until almost midnight. When it was time for Manuel to make his plane, they wouldn't hear of our using a taxi; they took us all. When Gert's plane left last night, they took us again and afterwards came in with me for some more study. I hope that they will become Bahá'ís. They are so beautiful. They have a nine-year-old son who is also in love with the Faith. I gave them all books and they are studying deeply. My prayers for them rock my soul. Manuel, with whom they fell in love, has promised to come to Bonaire at least once every two months to deepen with them and to work with the few other good contacts on the island. I feel so good about Bonaire. The postmaster, Marco Martis, listened very attentively to Manuel when I introduced them and I know Manuel will continue that contact. Also, the Chief of Police was very kind. It is so strange that very few of the people came whom I had wanted Gert to meet, nor could we locate them – but we found so many new ones, most of them people I had only casually mentioned the Faith to.

My heart is more than a little sad about leaving now. I know, without doubt, that just a few months more and Bonaire will be a strong little Bahá'í community. Jose and Crisma know my Boochie Statie very well and will look after him. Jose will also teach a friend at work who seems interested.

When I think of what Gert and I poured into Manuel and how Manuel received it and used it, I get all goose-bumpy. You wouldn't believe that he is a Bahá'í of just a few days. It is as if he has always known the Teachings – and he hasn't even been officially enrolled!

Now, in just four days, Tom will be here. I know that all our friends will fall in love with him too and he will share some of the wonder I have found.

When Manuel first came he was a little cocky about the superiority of the Curaçaoan people. It is true that they have much more of the material things in life than the Bonairians but, when he was leaving, he said that he hadn't realized that Bonairians were so beautiful, that they are so much kinder and gentler than Curaçaoans, and that he wished he could stay here. Gert suggested he try to sell his father the idea of opening a branch store here. Oh God, if that were possible Bonaire would lead the Faith in the Dutch Antilles! Please join me in prayers for my wonderful, beautiful, gentle, unspoiled Bonaire.

Dear friends, this will be the last letter from Bonaire. I'll probably do a summing up from Las Vegas. I understand from Tom's letters that we will be there for about six weeks. I know that there will be things to tell you concerning Tom's stay here – but I also know I will not make the time to write while he is here. So be patient, know that I love you all very dearly and shall never be able to tell you how much your letters have meant to me. They carried the love that flows across the continent and across ocean and sea to me. I feel that love very strongly. It has given me the courage, the patience and the strength to do what I had to do. In a very real sense, you were on this post with me and the glory and the bounty is yours.

Las Vegas
January 28, 1976

I HAVE been back in the States for just a little more than two weeks and it has been like stepping through a looking-glass or dropping down a rabbit hole. This life seems so unreal. Bonaire was more real and the woman who lived there and developed into the Mimi-person was the real person. In spite of the relaxed, casual, unplanned way of life on Bonaire, each day had more plan, more purpose and more order than any of the seventeen days since I've returned. I have tried very hard to pull my thoughts together and write the final chapter to the Bonaire story but it has been very difficult. There, I had so much to say – I was beginning to know who I was and to feel comfortable in that knowing. Back here, none of that Bonaire experience seems to have relevance. But because I feel I owe it to you who have been so patient with me, so understanding, so sympathetic, I shall try to write the finish. (Even as I write the word 'finish' I could cry).

Jose and Crisma Winklaar did not become Bahá'ís before I left. Crisma and Renato, her son, came to the airport to see us off and she brought me a little gift. We both cried. Rhoda was also at the airport so I had a chance to introduce Crisma to Rhoda and hope that the same kind of rapport will develop between them as we enjoyed.

Dulia Dortalina, my yoga teacher, had asked me the day before we left the island to be sure to stop by her house on the way to the airport. When we did she also had a gift for me and, again, in tears we clung to one another like departing lovers. It almost seemed like a betrayal to leave her at this point. It was almost as if, having planted a seed and exposing it to the sunshine, the water of the love of a warm personal contact was removed.

Tom and I saw the Louie Martis family several times but, on the day we left, we stopped by for a final visit. They wanted to take pictures of us and we of them. When we left, sweet, dear, gentle Mrs Martis shyly handed me a beautifully wrapped gift. Again, eyes misted and parting was difficult.

Tom was able to meet and have some good conversation with my good friend, Siegfried Pourrier, the councilman from Bonaire. Siegfried is a good friend of the Faith and has said that he is in deep sympathy with the Bahá'í Teachings. He has read all the literature Gert and I gave him. Bonaire is emerging from centuries of dependence and is straining towards autonomy. Siegfried, deeply involved in the political life of the island, will be one of the men who will help her achieve her freedom. He feels he must be single-minded at this time in his life and that single-mindedness must be for Bonaire. I shall continue to correspond with him.

Tom and I visited all of the close friends I had made and each visit was emotion-charged. I could hardly bear to leave them and they were reluctant to see me go. Tom felt, very strongly, the power of the love I shared with these people.

We visited Raphael at work and saw his mother and sister Poppi, at their home. We spent some time with Boochie, spoke to Josie Statie (not directly related to either of the other Staties) who works at the Bonaire Beach Coffee Hut. I took Tom to meet Doie, my taxi man, and his wife and, of course, Jacqueline.

Jacqueline was at the house as often as she could possibly be. I had to keep the door locked or she would have come at 7:00 in the morning – or earlier. I had got used to living in a kind of fish-bowl but I didn't think Tom should have to. The day before we left was a very sad day for Jacqueline. She almost clung and when, finally, I had to speak strongly to her and tell her we had packing to do and many things to take care of, she left – but not without looking back – and I can still see her rather homely, child face. She was trying so hard not to cry. She had asked me several times the day before if I really had to go. She couldn't – or wouldn't – understand why Rhoda had to come back and I had to leave. I'm afraid her final reaction was one of resentment and a feeling of having been betrayed. But again Jacqueline taught me a valuable lesson. A pioneer – or a travel teacher – must learn to be detached, not only from the past but the present, lest attachment interfere with the plans of the future.

February 17

MUCH time has passed since I began this last installment. Tom and I have moved our Airstream onto a pad in a trailer court and for the past several days I have been trying to put the remains of 40 years of life into the space provided by a trailer. I am discovering that the Bonaire experience has been invaluable. I am also realizing how very much I depended on my files of reference materials and the dozens of courses I have developed through the years. Tom may have to stay in southern Nevada for several weeks, possibly two months or more. I am trying to get things organized here so that if – God and the International Teaching Committee willing – I set out again on a project to teach the Faith, Tom will be able to manage.

February 22

IN Bonaire, after spending part of almost every day with Carlos, the last day was almost more than either he or I could take. Tom and I stayed a long while and joked and laughed and spoke of everything and nothing.

Finally I said, 'Well, Carlos, this is our last visit.'

Peevishly and crankily he replied, 'I know. I know.' His eyes began to fill. He tried hard not to cry so he turned to Tom and said, 'Mr West, Mr West,' but broke down and wept.

Tom and I were also broken up and I bent down and kissed the dear old man – with tears running down my cheeks. I gave him one last hug and left quickly.

Since I've been back, I've written to him twice and sent him some cash for his birthday which was February

22. (By gosh, that's today!) I've had a letter from Rhoda in which she says he got my first letter and wants to answer it himself. She said he is able to write quite well. He continues to be a great miracle to me. This is the man the doctor said would never get out of bed. I shall be eternally grateful to this valiant soul for confirming what I always have believed – that age need be no deterrent to human dignity, that the human spirit can rise above the indignities of age and pain. Carlos has reaffirmed my belief that there is no defeat for us save the acceptance of defeat.

I guess Boochie was the only disappointment. Unfortunately, the Christmas tourist rush kept him so busy at the airport that we had very little time to spend with him or to continue to deepen him. He also got caught up in the holiday festivities and his guilt feelings kept him from us. Rhoda's last letter indicated that she had met him. I pray that in time he may become more involved with the group.

As the plane carried us away from Bonaire, I began to exist on two levels. Part of me was joyous at the coming reunion with my family and the dear friends in Nevada. That part vibrated at the loving reunion with Tom and the knowledge that, for at least awhile, we would be together. But the other part – the Mimi part – suffered with the knowledge of such final separation from those new friends I had come to love so dearly and to whom I felt I owed so much.

There is no way for me to adequately express my gratitude for being able to experience Bonaire. I have learned many lessons during the past year – not the least of which is that I must school myself in the practice of detachment. To be detached from all save God is the road to sainthood and this poor bundle of human weaknesses realizes only too well that, for her, that goal is unattainable. But to learn enough detachment so that one's heart doesn't break at each parting – this should be possible. The only thing in this life that I really want to do, need to do, is to teach and spread the Message of Bahá'u'lláh. Call me a fanatic and I'll say, 'Thank you'. If the price of teaching in far-away places is the pain of separation, I must learn to welcome the pain – at least to feel the pain so little that I can be free.

Finally, I want to say that pioneering and travel-teaching may not be for everyone but until you have tried it, you will never know. But I wish I could deglamourize the whole thing and convince the friends that the most exciting thing they can do is to teach wherever they are. The excitement of teaching, the rewards of teaching should provide all the 'glamour' we need.

To find one soul and warm it with your love and gently turn it towards the Greatest Love, to watch it respond and grow, to be to it a prop and shelter in its weakness and fragility, this is the supreme excitement – and it can happen anywhere. This does not depend on distance. It's right next door. But if you get the chance to go 'out', go without fear. Go with glorious anticipation. May you all find your 'Bonaires'.

I send you all my love,

Mimi

A Postscript from Tom

February 26

EVER since Mimi asked me to write my impressions of Bonaire (one week), Curaçao (two days) and Aruba (half an hour) during my recent trip to the ABC Islands, I've been writing it mentally; but now that I've actually started it, my mind is as blank as this page was before I started hammering at it. Before I start actually writing I do want to tell you that all duplicating (my part), collating, stapling, folding, addressing, stamping and mailing these letters (Jane Ward's part) was a labor of love for you, the Faith and for Mimi . . . and it was a pleasure, too.

The air flight down was uneventful even though it was my first time out over the Caribbean . . . but I did get kind of a thrill flying over one tip of Cuba on one side (because I remembered that Viola Tuttle, Hand of the Cause Leroy Ioas's sister, and others from his family had pioneered there years ago) and Haiti on the other side (because I remembered the tremendous experience Ellsworth Blackwell had there with President Duvalier). And then, well after dark, we landed on Aruba and I spent my half hour nosing around the modern airport building. Then on to Curaçao where Mimi, Nosrat Rabbani (what a dear!), and Manuel Maduro, a new believer with a beartrap mind that has snapped onto the Message with a love and depth that is unbelievable, waited. He lavished his love on us in his home that night, the following day and night and the next morning (Sunday) when Mimi and I departed for Bonaire on the first plane available to us. You can well imagine the warmth and fervor of Mimi's and my meeting so I won't go into it except to say that in my eyes she was more beautiful than she was the day I married her . . . so slim and so tanned and so beautiful! Anyway, Mimi (my new-found Antillian) and I spent the two nights and a day and a half flitting around on Curaçao, mostly in the vicinity of Wilhelmstad, calling on many of the Bahá'ís, doing a little sightseeing on the way to and from, doing some teaching and deepening as the circumstances presented themselves, and finally, we cut a couple of tapes to be broadcast on Curaçao Radio by Rigoberto Melendrez, another new and exciting Bahá'í who is something of a linguist and wants to come to the States. All of this in a rented car with Manuel and Rigoberto as our guides and chauffeurs.

On to Bonaire. Of course, Mimi had done a PR job on us all in her letters, so I was prepared to *like* it, but as we flew in on that Sunday morning approach and the whole island, practically, was in panorama before my eyes, I fell in *love* with it, confirming my first impressions. Mimi, an old hand at landing at the little airport, could call off things as she pointed: 'the tanks – the church spire at Rincón – Klein Bonaire – the two 'little' tugs at their mooring – the salt pans – the Flamingo Beach Hotel where Raphael works – the beach, the Hut and the Hotel Bonaire itself' and on and on and finally, 'I wonder if Doie will be there to meet us?' And he was – warm and friendly and dependable. And so it was with all her friends: sweet and gentle people, concerned about you, how you were feeling, really glad to meet Mimi's '*casa*' ('husband' in Papiamentu, not 'house' as in Spanish), tickled when you said an expression in Papiamentu (the first one I learned was '*te aworo*' which means 'see you later'), ready to help satisfy any want or desire you might express. This *genuineness* not only made me deeply appreciate them as persons but served to greatly increase my endearment to their locale. And I met them all – but I can't go into detail because I have only this page. So I'll speak briefly about Carlos, the 86-year-old who *walked* so proudly for us (but for Mimi, mostly), who laughed and joked and, for the third time, proposed marriage to Mimi, this time in front of me! He was so jolly when we posed for pictures in the courtyard of the hospital – and so wiped out after his last goodbye to Mimi that all he could say to me was, 'Well, Mr West . . . ' (tears, sobs, expressions of woe and dejection). I'll never forget Bonaire and Carlos.

Epilogue

RETURNING to Nevada caused a kind of reverse culture shock. I looked in vain for the beautiful variety of skin colors that both my eyes and my soul had grown accustomed to enjoying. Life once again became frenetic and very soon, too soon, I was caught up in State-side living. But I discovered that I had learned to accept and adapt, that I could be pushed without feeling pushed, that I could be in a maelstrom and not feel frantic. Dear, gentle Bonaire had taught me well.

Tom and I settled down into the old familiar pattern of studying and teaching. Our work with the Indians of Northern Nevada continued to be a source of deep satisfaction. We had been successful in bringing into being the first all-Indian Assembly in Nevada and had been saddened to see its membership decimated by the passing of some of the older believers. We were trying to reactivate the Bahá'í community there.

I had been home for about four months when again a call from the National Bahá'í Center sent me out. This time it was to South Carolina to help establish an Assembly in the town of Mullins. Although hundreds of believers had been enrolled in that small town during the mass-teaching efforts in the south in the early '70s no assembly had been established. Once again, with Tom's full support, I spent three months away from him and did succeed in helping to form an Assembly before the end of the Bahá'í year.

Back home once again Tom and I began to make plans for his eventual retirement. His health, more fragile than mine, would not permit strenuous overseas pioneering but he was so eager to spread out and do some of the exciting travel teaching that I had done. We soon agreed to sell our home, invest in a big and travel-worthy mobile home and offer our services to the National Teaching Committee as a team working the western seaboard. We did, indeed, buy an Airstream and a ¾ ton truck to pull it and began to do what had to be done toward our goal. Tom still had a year to work until retirement.

But a nice quiet year with my husband was not meant to be for once again that phone call came and once again, 'How can you say no?' and off it was again. This time I had been asked to come to work at the National Teaching Committee Office at the National Center in Wilmette, Illinois. My job, initially, was to work with newly-formed and/or struggling young Assemblies. It was the kind of nurturing, guiding, teaching work I liked best and I was very excited by it. However, after I had been at the National Center for a few months a new direction was taken by the Teaching Committee and I became the Coordinator for the Western States which meant I worked not only with those Assemblies but with the committees and groups in the Western region.

I worked there for about a year and returned home with Tom who had come to get me. We drove back across the country talking and planning and dreaming of what lay ahead of us. We arrived back in Nevada in January of 1977 after having made many teaching stops en-route.

On the morning of March 30th, the day before Tom was to hand in his retirement papers, he left on a job-related trip to California. I wanted so much to go with him and shamelessly nagged him to take me. But I was barely recovering from a severe cold and Tom insisted I stay home and go back to bed after he left. I did and slept until about a little before 1:00 when I was awakened by what I thought was Tom coming in the front door. I got up to greet him and was surprised to find the door still locked from the inside and no evidence that Tom had come home. It was so much earlier than I had expected him that I reasoned that I had been dreaming and put it out of my mind.

About 4:00 that afternoon two people came to my door and asked if they might come in. One had a very official-looking badge on. When they had come inside I was asked to sit down because they had some bad news to tell me.

Tom had been killed on the road to his appointment.

Stunned, not yet comprehending, not yet believing, I asked 'When did this happen?'

The time of death had been about 1:00 p.m. A truck had run into him head-on and he had been killed instantly. All doubts dispelled, I knew Tom had gone. I knew beyond all doubt that my beloved, my other self, had let me know what I didn't want to know.

Through the difficult time which followed I was sustained by a small verse from the Writings of our Faith. I learned it well, and shall never be without it:

> Ask not of Me that which We desire not for thee, then be content with what We have ordained for thy sake, for this is that which profiteth thee, if therewith thou shalt content thyself.

After the funeral, my daughter and son-in-law moved me down to Southern Nevada where they were living. There was really no reason for me to stay up north. While my friends, Bahá'í and non-Bahá'í, were dear to me, I agreed that I needed my children and grandchildren very much at this time. Maxine, my daughter, Billy, my son-in-law and I helped strengthen the North Las Vegas Assembly until we moved to Boulder City to be the seventh, eighth and ninth members of that newly-formed Assembly.

The teachings of our Faith tell us that we are as close to the next world as the child in the womb is to this world and that we should pray for those who have departed EVEN AS THEY PRAY FOR US. I redoubled my teaching efforts assured that Tom would be adding his efforts to mine and that I would still be serving for both of us.

During the years which followed I visited Jamaica, England and Wales, and the Leeward and Windward Islands on teaching trips. In 1979, almost ten years after Tom and I had made our pilgrimage to the Bahá'í Holy Places in Haifa, Israel, I made a second pilgrimage. It was a time of healing, of fulfillment and of renewal.

I am currently engaged in something which gives me great satisfaction. I am counselling a Widow/Widowers Support Group at the Boulder City Senior Centre and also doing private counselling. I have discovered a talent for this so have gone back to school for some more courses. We have had some wonderful breakthroughs in the group. One dear old man aged 86 said that for the first time since the death of his wife, two-and-a-half years ago, he is without guilt. He no longer has to ask himself what he did wrong or whether he could have done more. When I started with the group, everyone was so sad and solemn. Now we laugh and share stories and have a buddy system working. The group has grown in number from four to eighteen. It may be necessary to start another group. I couldn't have done this without the experience of my own loss and learning how to cope with it.

Am I reconciled to losing him? No. I still ache for him, I miss his gentleness and his quick wit and humor. I miss not being able to share the victories and the set-backs. I still need the reassurance that I can do whatever the Faith requires of me. But I am a happy woman.

Teaching the Faith in Bonaire meant a long period of separation from my husband, but I would not have missed the experience for all the money in the world or any title the Faith could bestow. I shall always love Bonaire and love it dearly for it was here that I really found out who and what Marion West is.